HELMETS AND LIPSTICK

RUTH G. HASKELL
2nd Lieutenant A.N.C,

First published by G. P. Putnam's Sons in 1944

This edition published in 2017.

Table of Contents

TO MY SON

Preface

Usually when one thinks of the Army in times such as these, a picture comes to mind of a stalwart group of fighting soldiers striding off to war. It is very true that Uncle Sam has many, many nephews in his service, but in these past three years he has also acquired many nieces. Included among the latter are the Army nurses. These are the girls who are striving to take the best care possible of your sons, husbands, and sweethearts. Our need for many more of these girls is urgent, and this book is intended to tell a bit about the trials and tribulations, the fun and the thrills, to be experienced as a member of the Corps. I personally wouldn't have missed the experience for anything I know of, and I am sure there are others who will feel the same way when this conflict is over and we are a nation at peace again.

Ruth G. Haskell, 2nd Lieut. A.N.C.

CHAPTER ONE: Orders for Foreign Service

It all began with a telephone call. The sharp whir of the bell broke the silence of the hot Tennessee afternoon. I lazily reached for the receiver, still checking the chart on which I was working.

"A-15, Lieutenant Haskell speaking."

"Lieutenant Haskell, this is it! You are relieved of duty as of now. Come to the office for your clearance papers. Clear the post. You are to be in New York not later than midnight on Monday." This was the crisp voice of First Lieutenant Marion Harvey, assistant to the chief nurse.

"Yes, ma'am," I answered meekly, placed the receiver carefully in its cradle, and sat there in a complete daze.

Foreign service! I had volunteered about a month before, but now that the orders were actually here, I found I was a little panicky about the whole thing. It was a thing we all talked about but thought of as being in the dim, dark future. I hastily finished what I was doing, said goodbye to my patients, not without some regrets, and dashed madly across the ramp to the nurses' quarters.

Anyone who has ever lived in the Deep South will know what I mean when I say my room was like an oven. I remember thinking it couldn't be much worse out of doors, so I decided to clear the post first. I ran a comb through my hair, dusted a little powder on my nose, and reported to the Chief Nurse's office.

As I entered the office, Kate Rodgers, the camp glamour girl, was going in just ahead of me.

"Where are my clearance papers?" she asked of Lieutenant Moat.

"Are you going, too?" I asked in a rather astonished manner.

"Before I change my mind, I hope," she replied. "This seemed a rather good idea a few weeks ago, but now I don't know!"

I could appreciate what she meant, because secretly I was feeling the same way.

Lieutenant Moat handed each of us a sheaf of papers and explained what they were for. It seemed we had to be signed off the post by all the various departments to vouch for the fact we didn't owe the government any money.

"Am I late?" This was the voice of Margaret Hart of Bristol, Tennessee. "Thought I never would get off duty. We certainly have been having a busy day in the O.K."

Marjie, as we called her, was a contradiction if ever I saw one. Vivacious, good-looking, and a beautiful dancer, always in the throes of either falling in or out of love, she was a marvelously efficient operating-room nurse. This fact had never ceased to amaze everyone who knew her.

Just as we turned to leave the office, Lieutenant Moat asked, "Do any of you know anything about Mildred Harris? She signed for this thing too and she is on leave. I'm not sure where I can reach her."

We all grinned at each other, thinking about what Millie's reaction would be if she found her, because she had been trying for some time to get home on leave.

Just about the time Marjie started to answer her, in dashed Eleanor Faulk. She, too, it seems, was looking for her clearance papers. Lieutenant Moat repeated her question regarding Mildred; Eleanor thought for a second, and then: "Oh, yes, she is visiting with relatives in Rome, Georgia. But I don't know just where."

At this point I began to wonder if I might just possibly be going to be the only Northerner in an entire "Rebel" group.

"How many of us are leaving?" I asked.

"Let me see," looking back at the list before her. "There are five of you. Mildred Harris, Eleanor Faulk, Kate Rodgers, Margaret Hart, and yourself." She began to smile as she told me this, as though she might be thinking the same thing.

The four of us started back for the barracks, and as we walked along we discussed the problem of Lieutenant Moat finding Millie in time to get her started off with us as it was mid-afternoon on Saturday and time was short.

"Listen here," said Eleanor. "I don't see any sense in all of us running around in this heat. Why don't two of us take these confounded papers around and get them signed?"

Rodgers and Hart looked quickly at each other and smiled and I thought: They certainly have something up their sleeves.

Kate spoke up. "I certainly would appreciate it if I didn't have to go. I have a date for the officers' club tonight."

"So have I," chimed in Marjie.

I looked at Eleanor to see what she was going to add, but she looked rather preoccupied and wasn't paying any attention to what was being said.

"I'll take them if someone will come with me. I'm not sure where all these places are. Where is the Signal Corps headquarters, and why do they have to sign us out?"

I couldn't see any sense in going there or to the camp bakery, but it seemed that the Army thought we should, so we didn't have anything to say about it, I guess.

Finally Eleanor and I sadly started off in the heat to get the darned things signed. It was Saturday, and about a third of the people we had to see weren't in. Time was going, and we still had all our packing to do. We returned to the barracks and, much to our disgust, found Kate and Marjie all freshened up, manicured, shampooed, and rested.

"Are you packed?" I asked.

"Yes, Madge packed for us. We're all set. Isn't that fine?"

I muttered something about some people having all the luck and stalked off toward my own room. About the time I arrived there, Pauline Loignon, a girl from home, came in, and the look on her face was something to behold. She and I had come into the Army the same day and had become fast friends. Evidently she had just heard that I had received my orders, and she was much upset about it.

"What am I going to do without you?" she asked. "You know how much I depend on you. I don't want you to go, do you hear?"

"Pauline, honey, in two weeks time you'll never know I existed. Stop your fussing and start helping me pack!"

We finally got busy and I began to see my way clear to being able to get to bed some time before midnight. I still wonder who in the world besides myself could possibly have acquired all the junk I seemed to have collected from somewhere. The worst of it was, I didn't want to dispose of any of it. I swear I would have packed the dusty old corsages I took down off the wall if Pauline hadn't thrown them into the wastebasket first.

Late that night as I tried to get ready to sleep, and goodness knows by that time I was ready to, I began to think of all the friends I had made in the past fourteen months and of how much I was going to miss them. Camp Forrest, Tullahoma, Tennessee. I grinned to myself in the dark when I remembered how I had hunted frantically on the map for the place when I first received my orders to report there. That is one sad thing about army friendships, you meet so many people, learn to like them, and then away one or the other goes and you never see them again.

Sunday morning! When I first wakened I couldn't imagine what my trunk was doing there in the middle of the room and packed to overflowing. Then I remembered, this was the day! I lay there a few seconds blinking into the sunlight and wondered what the next month, or even the next week, might bring. I began to wonder about the other four girls and whether or not we would get along. Kate was from Houston, Texas. Slim, pretty, almost Spanish-looking with her black hair and shining dark eyes. She was exceedingly popular with the officers on the post, danced beautifully, and was much in demand socially. She had the knack of getting things done for her rather than doing them for herself, just from the pure force of her personality. As it developed, she had Madge, our colored maid, do her packing for her while the rest of us slaved away at our own.

Marjie was tall, a striking brunette, extremely well proportioned. She appeared to be rather young and not entirely sure of her own mind, although, as I have said before, she was a very good nurse. Her chief hobby in life seemed to be the number of scalps she could collect from the poor helpless males. Her home was in Bristol, Tennessee, and she certainly was the typical Southern belle.

Mildred was a slim little thing, determined and emphatic about her likes and dislikes, and with a temper that flew off at a tangent at the most unexpected times and places. She was a loyal friend if she liked you, and made no bones of letting you know it if she didn't. As I thought of her, I wondered if Lieutenant Moat had been able to reach her, and I smiled to myself as I imagined what she would say if called back from her leave. Her home was somewhere in Georgia, and I often wondered what sort of place it might be.

Eleanor was a type all her own. Her hair was dark brown and reached her waist. She wore it braided and wound around her head coronet fashion. Her nose and cheeks were sprinkled liberally with freckles, which she disliked very much but which served to make her very attractive. She had a rather driving, dynamic personality, evidently used to getting her own way. There were many times when one could shake her for being so very sure of herself, but the damning part of it was that she was almost always right! Her home was in Memphis, Tennessee, and I think, all in all, she was the most likable girl of the gang.

"Well, lazybones! Are you going to sleep all morning?"

I got up on my elbow to see who was speaking, and there stood Marianna Smith with a tray. It seemed they were to make a lady of me my last day and give me breakfast in bed!

"Get out of there and enjoy this while it's hot," she said as she plopped herself down on the foot of my bed.

"You know, don't you, that you are going to be missed around here?" She looked rather serious for a second, and then: "In a way I wish I were going, too, but I guess I can't just make up my mind what I want to do and when!"

"I rather think I'm going to be lonely for all my Camp Forrest friends, too. You know, folks have been darned nice to me around here."

Some way or other I managed to finish all the last minute things one has to do when packing. I looked around the little boxlike room that had been my home for the past fourteen months and wondered what the future would bring. If I had only known!

"Ruth, you are wanted on the telephone. You are going to have dinner with us in the mess hall today, aren't you?" asked Pauline.

"Yes, honey, I sure am. I'm glad it's fried chicken. Lord only knows when I'm apt to get another one." I walked over to the telephone. "Lieutenant Haskell speaking," I said.

"Lieutenant Haskell, this is the Chief Nurse. There will be transportation for you girls to go to the station at two-forty-five. Be at Quarters One at that time. Your reservations are all made, and your luggage will be picked up shortly after lunch."

I thanked her, and as I hung up the receiver I had a very funny feeling about this really being terribly final as far as my life at Camp Forrest was concerned.

Two-forty-five, and a station wagon rolled up to the door of Quarters One. I think in a way we were all relieved, because we were a little upset, emotionally, at the many goodbyes to be said.

We were all rather proud of the way we looked. We were wearing, for the first time that summer, the beige uniform of the Army Nurse Corps, and feeling for the first time as though we might really be part of the Army. Up to that time, uniforms had not been compulsory and we wore civies when off duty.

Lieutenant Moat had given Eleanor instructions for the entire group and last-minute orders to remember that we were part of the Army and that we must always be a credit to the uniform.

"I'll say goodbye to you here as I feel you should start out on this responsible trip entirely on your own. Good luck to you. Keep well. I know I shall always be proud of you, wherever you may be!" With this remark Lieutenant Moat shook our hands, gave us a hurried pat on the shoulder, and left.

"Come on, you kids, we'll be late, you haven't got all day!" This from Ruth Jones, a very attractive girl from Philadelphia who had been a close friend of mine for many months.

"I'll see you at the station," sang out Kathryn Goodman.

Finally we climbed into the station wagon, and as we drove around the circle in front of headquarters I wondered if we would ever be back there again.

"What about our foot lockers?" asked Eleanor of the driver.

"Everything that I own is in it and I'm darned sure I don't want to lose track of mine, do you?" This was little Millie speaking (yes, Lieutenant Moat had reached her, and Rome, Georgia, was not too far away).

"They are all at the station and are to be shipped through on your tickets. Don't worry about them. They will be there when you arrive." Thus spoke the driver of the vehicle as we drove up into the yard of the station.

It being hot enough almost to cook a gal, I for one was glad when we saw the locomotive of the good old Chattanooga Choo-Choo rounding the bend. Everybody who had come to see us off kissed us goodbye (even a few soldiers who were just innocent bystanders! Guess they thought it was like a wedding, where everybody kissed the bride!).

"Write to me soon. I hate to write letters, but I promise I'll answer every one I receive." Jonesy looked a little bright around the eyes as she said this.

I laughed and hugged her close to me.

"See you in Timbuktu or some other fine place. You will be following us soon."

(You can imagine my surprise when I came face to face with her in Algeria some five months later!)

We pulled slowly out of the small town of Tullahoma, and as we looked back at the barracks of camp fading from sight, we all became very quiet. Guess we realized how many good friends we were leaving behind, and our minds were crowded with memories of all the fun we had enjoyed there.

Several hours passed. Each of us had apparently been lost in thought about personal problems.

"I'm hungry," Eleanor said. "What do you say we go into the diner for a bite to eat?"

"Fine, I didn't realize I was so hungry. What about the rest of you girls, are you coming with us?" Marjie stepped out into the aisle and started down toward the end of the car.

"Why don't we all go?" I asked, and promptly followed the other two girls.

We enjoyed a fine dinner, for which we paid just about enough to buy the train, and returned to our seats to read for a while before the porter made up our berths.

We arrived in Washington the next morning, and as we came back through the train from having breakfast in the diner, we passed another group of about six girls who were gazing out of the window in a very disconsolate manner. I recognized the Nurse Corps insignia on the collar of one of the girls' shirts.

"Excuse me, but aren't you Army nurses too?" I smiled at one of the girls and hesitated by the seat.

The rest of the girls had gone on ahead, so I sat on the arm of the seat to talk to them for a second. It was a boiling hot day, and I felt badly for them because they were wearing their winter woolens and I was nearly dead in a Palm Beach cloth suit!

"We are from Camp Wheeler, Georgia," volunteered one of the group.

I replied that we were from Camp Forrest down in Tennessee. "I imagine," I added, "you are going to the same place we are."

One of the girls seemed willing to talk and visit, but the others were rather distant. Finally I asked her if she wouldn't like to join us back in the other car, and along she came.

"You know, I didn't ask to come on this safari." She looked a little indignant. "I've only been in the Army a couple months and didn't expect orders for foreign service for some time. Oh, well, I guess it doesn't make much difference as long as I have to go sometime anyway."

This girl was Louise Miller, a winsome little blonde from Selma, Alabama. I instinctively liked her. She was frail and, like myself, of average height with fair complexion.

I was much surprised that she had received orders without volunteering for the mission. She told us that not enough girls had volunteered to go, so their chief nurse had just picked two girls to fill the quota.

Soon she returned to her friends and we began to gather our things together, as we were due into the city in a very short time.

Orders for our group read: Report to the Port of Embarkation. Mildred Harris was the only girl in the group who knew New York at all. I had been there a couple of times with patients and had gone up to the World's Fair the year it opened. But I certainly didn't feel I knew enough about the city to find my way around — to say nothing of getting the gang of us to the port.

After much discussion we decided to taxi to the Army Base, and so we piled the five of us, luggage and all, into one of the ubiquitous Yellow Cabs and off we started on what was to prove an adventure. In the first place the cab driver was strictly a Manhattan product, and after he got out of the midtown district he didn't know where he was, and neither did we! He seemed much amazed that we knew where we wanted to go but didn't know how to get there. Finally, after riding back and forth and around and about, we arrived at the front gate of the Army Base with an armed guard walking slowly back and forth giving everybody suspicious looks. It seems you are definitely wrong until you prove you have a right to be there. We all had passes of the regular Army type, the kind that has a picture of you pasted on it that looks more like your old maid aunt than it does like you. We finally convinced the guard that we had business there, and he let us through the turnstile. Of course on the way through I practically had the suitcase torn out of my hand. Just a little gal from the country!

We walked into a large barnlike building. Finally we came across another soldier with a gun over his shoulder.

"Say, soldier, where is the Chief Nurse's office around here?"

He grinned in a condescending manner and told us to take the elevator to the third floor and, when we got there, to ask for Lieutenant Witter's office.

Finally, after following instructions, we arrived in a huge room on one side of which dozens of soldiers and girls sat at typewriters working like mad. A little farther on were about fifty nurses looking as if they had lost their last boy friend. We finally located the Chief Nurse, and Eleanor passed over the envelope containing our written orders. She looked them over hurriedly and waved us on to where girls in groups of four or five were writing at several small tables.

"I wonder what those girls are doing?" asked Kate.

"I don't know, but I imagine we'll soon find out. Let's go over and ask. Probably we have to do the same thing."

With this remark Eleanor led the way over to the nearest group of girls who were standing around looking as puzzled as we were. It developed that this particular group were from Fort Knox, Kentucky.

"What are all these girls writing?" asked Mildred. "Do we have to do it, too?"

At this point the Chief Nurse came to our assistance.

"All you girls who have just arrived come over to this section of the room and we'll explain how you are to make out your insurance and allotment papers."

About the time we got it through our thick heads what we were to do to the various forms we were given to fill out, another girl came bustlingly over to us and said,

"If you are finished, you are to come out back to the dispensary and have your shots."

"Shots! What kind of shots?" we all chorused as one.

"Tetanus, typhus, and typhoid!"

"All at once?" we cried.

"Certainly," she smiled sweetly. "You are in the Army now, or didn't you know?"

With that remark we felt there was very little left to say, so we just followed her — not without some fears, for we had heard many an enlisted man rave about the "assembly line" method of inoculations.

We all stood in line and one by one received our shots. The medical men who were giving them to us were as impersonal as though they were sticking a hypo needle into an orange (as we had been taught to do early in our training days). They looked down our throats, listened to our chests, tapped us here and there, and pronounced us physically fit for whatever was ahead of us.

By this time we were getting pretty tired, but it seemed we had only just begun! We lined up again, this time to receive our issue of field equipment. Holy cats! First we received a sack-like affair that they told us was a musette bag, and then a belt with a container hanging from it that was to be our source of drinking water from there on in. When they passed me some sort of gadget that looked like a frying pan with a cover, they told me that it was my mess kit! That didn't mean a thing, then, but I certainly found out it was a mess in more ways than one before the next ten months were out.

"Have you girls received your bedding rolls?" asked Lieutenant Witter.

We looked a little puzzled. We had no idea what she was talking about.

"I guess you haven't, if I am to judge by the very intelligent look on your faces!" With this remark, she spoke to a soldier who was standing near by and told him to take us along with him and to see that we received a bedding roll and were taught how to roll it.

First we were given a huge canvas-like affair with three huge straps on it. The soldier spread mine out on the floor, and we discovered that there were two pockets on each end of the thing and that the sides folded over and strapped before it was rolled. I was still in doubt as to what it was when the soldier said,

"Have you anything you want to pack in this?"

"What in heaven's name is it? What do you mean, do we have anything to pack in it?"

He gave me a withering and pitying look, and I began to feel properly squelched.

"This, my dear Lieutenant, is your bed and your trunk all in one. You pack your clothing flat under your blankets, always arranging it so that when you open the thing it is ready to sleep in. The pockets are for your shoes and small equipment, and you must interfold your blankets for warmth. You are a field soldier now."

About two hours later we emerged from that room perspiring and hot and tired, but with more than a vague idea what a bedding roll was and at least some idea how to roll the thing so that it wouldn't fall apart the first time it was picked up from the floor.

At this point I had begun to wonder if we were ever to get anything else to eat, but it seems that was the least of our worries. We were soon herded into one small room to have gas masks issued. August in New York, and we spent the greater part of another hour trying on face pieces of various types of gas masks to see if they fitted. Personally, I didn't see what the difference was between one that didn't fit and one that did, but there was a very stern gentleman wandering about with a birdie on his shoulder who seemed to think that there was a difference. I think we signed for the things and left just before he decided we were a group of mentally incurables.

"Young ladies, step over to this section and sign up for your helmets."

That did it. As we entered that room, a smart-looking corporal planked a helmet down on my already aching head, grinned, and swung me around to the mirror. Ye gods, I knew I wasn't anything to look at, but the face I saw reflected there was enough to scare children.

"That isn't exactly a Knox model, miss, but you will find that it is a comforting sort of thing to have between your head and any stray shells or shrapnel. Besides, it makes a grand washbasin."

When we had signed about a million forms and received enough equipment to take care of a small army, we were told to report back there at six-thirty the following morning. We were told also that our foot lockers would be at the hotel and we should have them completely packed and ready to be picked up early the next day.

Finally we hopped a cab and arrived at the hotel. We must have presented a pretty picture. We entered the lobby with gas masks slung over one shoulder, musette bag over the other, and carrying our suitcases, canteen belts, and helmets. Leave it to a New York hotel clerk to be blasé, for this one didn't bat an eyelash when we registered.

"Have you foot lockers in the baggage room for Lieutenants Haskell, Faulk, Harris, Hart, and Rodgers?"

The clerk called the baggage room, only to tell us that our lockers were not there as yet. That rather staggered us, as we had traveled in summer uniform, and our wools that we would have to wear on board ship were in our lockers with our overcoats and sweaters.

Marjie and I were assigned to room together and were taken to a room on the sixth floor. We dropped down onto the bed from sheer exhaustion before the bellhop had time to get the door closed.

"Ruth, aren't you terrified at the thought of that ocean trip?" Marjie asked.

"I hadn't thought about an ocean trip," I confessed, "to say nothing of Uncle Sam paying for one for me." I fell to wondering what kind of sailor I'd be.

We went to sleep without bothering to get anything to eat, and all too soon the desk clerk called and told us it was six o'clock. We asked if the lockers had ever been delivered to the hotel, and she informed us that as yet nothing had come for us. We really began to be concerned about it then, and wondered what we would do about the uniform situation.

As soon as we reported back to the Port of Embarkation we told the Chief Nurse that we didn't have our lockers. She looked rather annoyed and said she would have them checked on from the Tennessee end of the trip and see if they had ever been put onto the train.

We spent another two hours getting registered here and there, and then Lieutenant Witter came and told us our lockers had not been put on the train and wouldn't arrive in New York until after we were due to sail. She took us to the storeroom and issued us uniforms and warm clothing for the ocean trip, and we had to put our pretty beige uniforms into the confounded bedding rolls, and I think we were pretty well satisfied we had seen the last of our belongings. I was very unhappy, because I had had my uniform altered to fit and the one I was issued was a forty-two chest measure and I wore a thirty-eight.

About noon we were told that the afternoon was ours to do with as we wished, that we mustn't make any long-distance calls to our parents or boy friends, and that we mustn't send any telegrams that might give out any information as to the troop movement in the offing. We were told to report back by eight the next morning ready to go on board the transport.

That evening our group went out to have a final fling. We went into a restaurant just before returning to the hotel and decided to order what we wanted to eat no matter what it cost. You could almost tell where we were from by what we ordered.

"I'll have fried chicken," chorused the Rebels.

"Make mine a sea food plate," said I, a stern New Englander.

It didn't work with the dessert course, though, as we all settled eagerly for watermelon.

Back to the hotel and to bed. Tomorrow would be the day, and we were all too excited to sleep.

CHAPTER TWO: We Go for a Boat Ride

"COME ON, Marjie, it's time to get up. We've a date with the Army today, and somehow I don't think we'd better be late." With this remark I swung my pajama-clad legs over the side of the bed and staggered sleepily toward the bathroom. I remember wondering, as I stood there under the needle-like spray, where I would be likely to take my next shower — and when.

"I don't want to get up," protested Marjie, petulantly. "As far as I'm concerned, Haskell, six-thirty only comes in the afternoon."

"But this, my little chickadee," said I from the shower, "is the day we go for a boat ride. Remember?"

There was a lazy yawn from the bedroom.

"Oh, all right. All right. Get out from under that thing so I can get in."

In a short time we joined the rest of the group in the foyer of the hotel. It was terribly hot, and we were dressed in our winter blues with gas masks, canteens, musette bags, and what have you, all over us. Needless to say, we were anything but comfortable. Eventually we checked in at the Army Base and arrived upstairs just in time to receive orders to go back down again and line up for the march to the ferry which was to take us to the transport.

"My head aches," said Kate. "Besides, I don't see any sense in wearing all this collateral right here in New York." With this remark she gave her helmet a shove back on her head, only to have it promptly drop down over the bridge of her nose. Poor Kate. I thought: Well, darling, you may have had Madge do your packing for you, but you sure as blazes are going to have to wear your own helmet.

We stood there in formation, a very unmilitary-looking lot. I don't believe anyone had a very comfortable-fitting uniform, and we were all a bit nervous and apprehensive. That was a very deep and wide-looking ocean out there, from where we stood.

"Well, girls, good luck to you. We have only known you for a few hours but I'm sure you are the sort of girls who will go over there and do the job you have volunteered to do, and do it well. Keep well, and remember you live in the finest nation on this earth. Be a credit to that nation, the uniform that you wear, and most of all to yourselves. May God watch over and keep you, one and all." The Assistant Chief Nurse finished speaking and smiled at us, the sort of smile that just seems to enfold you in its sincerity.

"Attention — forward march." With this order we fell into line and started the long hike which would bring us to the dock.

There was the sound of a long-drawn-out whistle, and we looked up to see a large number of soldiers hanging out of the windows and grinning their heads off. I imagine we did present a funny sight with all that equipment just hanging off us, and most of us out of step, but even at that we didn't quite appreciate being laughed at. Later we learned to whistle right back, but at that time we were exceedingly annoyed.

As we lumbered along toward the harbor under the load of assorted equipment we could look up and see the old Statue of Liberty stood there in all her glory as though she were watching over her children. Soon we bumped and banged against the side of the transport, which appeared to be a rather large affair, and then the trek up the gangplank started. Our luggage had been carried on board for us, but we all felt rather weighed down by what we had on our backs. An officer stopped us and asked us our names, and gave us a stateroom number and told us how to get there.

"What's your stateroom number, Eleanor?" asked Millie.

"Sixty-four on A deck. What's yours?"

"Why, that's my number too," chorused Marjie and Kate together.

Just then I received a card bearing the same number, so it looked as though the Camp Forrest five were to stick together for the time being. After a fashion we reached A deck and Stateroom 64. The transport had evidently been one of our luxury liners before being converted into a troop ship, and the stateroom was a beautiful one with all the niceties removed. It seemed there were to be six of us to a room originally intended for three. There were three regular beds in the room, one of them a second-story bunk, and three regular Army cots, the canvas folding kind.

"This one is mine," announced Eleanor, throwing her luggage on the bed nearest the portholes.

"I want to be next to you," said Millie, and she chose the cot next to Eleanor's bed.

"This one looks all right to me. First come, first served," and I dropped my things down on the other bed. That left two cots and the upper bunk. Soon Marjie and Kate wandered in, and as they were discussing the sleeping arrangements, a slim, rather attractive-looking girl with light brown hair and blue eyes stood in the door, smiled hesitantly, and said:

"Guess I'm your other roommate. I'm Dora Kirkwood from Cincinnati."

We introduced ourselves, and all sat there smoking and getting acquainted when another girl came swiftly into file room.

"Kirk, are you in here?"

"Yes, I am, hon, come in and meet the girls. Girls, this is Glenna Whitt, my friend from Fort Thomas." With this remark she drew Glenna forward into the room.

I rather liked this new girl. Her personality was instantly pleasing, and she certainly was lovely to look at. Large dark brown eyes, and a short curly hair-do that stood out like a little girl's all over her head. It seemed that her home was in West Virginia, and it was evident that she and Kirk, as she called her, were fond of each other.

Soon Lieutenant Leona Henry, a girl from Camp Tyson, Tennessee, who had been made our chief nurse at the Port of Embarkation, came in to see how we were making out and to tell us that lunch would be served in a short time in the officers' mess on the deck above. She seemed to be a likable person although a little on the quiet side.

Soon we went upstairs to the lounge to await the serving of the noonday meal. As we stood grouped together, laughing and talking, many of the officers came over and introduced themselves, asked us where we were from, and generally entered into the conversation. Suddenly the whole thing began to take on all the aspects of a beautiful pleasure cruise. I smiled inwardly to see our Kate and Marjie measuring the poor unsuspecting males, one against the other, to decide which one they might be going to concentrate on while on board ship.

Soon the door of the dining room opened and out stepped a colored boy, rather small in stature and displaying a set of astonishingly white teeth as he grinned and swung the dinner bell. We passed slowly into the dining room well aware of the fact that some three hundred men had their eyes on us, and for that matter there weren't many of us missing a thing as far as they were concerned. After all, we were starting off for the Lord only knew where, and I guess we thought the trip might as well be enjoyed as long as we were obliged to go on it.

After enjoying what proved to be a delicious lunch, we all wandered out on deck to watch the loading of the hold. I must confess I held my breath at some of the loads that the huge cranes picked up off the dock and lowered down into the bowels of the ship. It didn't seem possible it could be done and the whole thing arrive intact.

"Good afternoon," said a young naval officer. "My name is Dick Travers. I hope you young ladies are going to enjoy your trip with us." He smiled a bit and then wrinkled his nostrils. "This is the nicest-smelling troop ship I've shipped on in some time. What is that exotic perfume you are wearing?" Apparently our tiny Millie had taken his eye.

"The name of it is Indiscreet." She blushed prettily as the rest of us howled with laughter.

"I'll bet you are from the South. You'd have to be, with such a slur in your speech."

"And I'll bet you are from the New England states," I challenged. "Am I right?"

It developed he had gone to college in a Massachusetts town and had lived a major part of his life in that particular part of the country.

"What's the idea, Dick?" asked a very good-looking young ensign. "Trying to keep all the nicest girls to yourself?"

"This is Mac, girls. Don't mind anything he says, he just flatters everybody. Guess it's his curly hair that gets them."

In the meantime several other officers joined our group and were introduced around, and then they proceeded to take us over the entire ship. That is one thing about getting to know the officers of the ship, one doesn't miss anything they are allowed to see. As we wandered along the sun deck, the strains of a victrola reached our ears and we came around upon our Kate doing a rhumba with an exceedingly Latin-looking naval lieutenant. They could certainly dance, and it was a joy just to watch them. As the record drew to a close, Kate discovered us standing there.

"Hello gang, lookee what I found!" and she flashed her most enticing smile up at him.

I thought: Boy, you may not know it, but you are elected to keep our Kate happy for the duration of the voyage or until she sees someone who interests her more than you do.

Then one of the members of the crew came and told us our commanding officer wanted to see us in the foyer off our sleeping quarters. This was the first time our curiosity had been aroused about the Commanding Officer, and as we wandered in from the deck to wait in the foyer, there was much speculation as to who he would be and whether we would like him.

Soon it developed that we were a surgical unit, or hospital, and that our work would carry us well into "hot" territory when the time came for us to do the job we came for. It seemed that the medical officers and enlisted men had been working together as a unit for some eighteen months in an Army camp in the Midwest. We learned that the Commanding Officer was from Illinois, a great big, genial, smiling lieutenant colonel by the name of Ringer. He was very pleasant as he introduced the rest of the medical officers to us and explained how we would work once we got set up in the field.

"Girls," he explained, "you are suddenly finding yourselves in the very real game of war. I know it has seemed like a beautiful cruise up to now, and I notice you aren't going to lack male attention. Go ahead and enjoy yourselves and have fun. Do not forget to conduct yourselves as ladies and officers. Relax and laugh, but don't forget it is important to obey orders without question, and never relax your vigilance once we are actually at sea. Wear your canteen belts at all times. The colored boys in the mess will fill your canteens once a day, and this must suffice as drinking water and as water for cleaning your teeth, as the water that comes from the taps in your staterooms is not potable. Do not leave your stateroom at any time without your canteen full of water. If anything should happen to the ship, that water might have to last you for some time in a lifeboat. Slacks and sweaters will be regulation uniform while on shipboard, and you must sleep in your clothes at night. When you return to your staterooms you will notice a small card just inside the door by the light switch. This has on it the number of your lifeboat station. Look at it — memorize it — think about it until you know it so well that there would be no question as to where you are to go if anything should necessitate our having to abandon ship. We will no doubt put to sea sometime in the early morning. You are to come here directly after dinner tonight to have your life belts issued to you. Once you have received a life belt, you are never to leave your room without it, and it is to be within reach the entire time that you are in your bunk. We are playing for keeps now, and the soldier, nurse, or officer who learns to do things the right way now will be the one who will be able to get along if worst comes to worst." With these words he turned on his heel and departed.

As we left the dining room, we were rather a subdued lot. What had seemed a lark a few hours before had all of a sudden assumed gigantic proportions. We had all realized we would be in more or less danger, but few people know how they are going to react to a given situation until they are faced with it. Most of us returned to our staterooms, although a few went back out on deck just as though they were not concerned in the least with all the things that the Colonel had just told us.

I dropped down onto my bunk, but my mind was entirely too alert to think of sleep. I had adjusted all my personal affairs before I left home so that my small son and family would be adequately taken care of, but as I lay there with my eyes closed I sort of wished that, at times, I hadn't been quite so thoughtless and selfish and that I had let my mother and dad know that I thought they were just about the best parents a girl ever had. It's the truest saying in the world, that we don't appreciate what we have until we feel in danger of losing it.

The bell rang for dinner, and we joined the rest of our group. We found that permanent places had been assigned for us in the mess. The girl who sat on my right was named Doris Brittingham, and she came from Wilmington, Delaware. Next to her was her pal Emily Nickerson, also from Wilmington. These girls had been through nurse's training together and had been stationed at Fort Slocum together before leaving for overseas. I was to grow very fond of them both in the months to come.

After dinner we retired to the lounge to await the Colonel and Chief Nurse and the issue of the life belts. Here the inevitable poker and blackjack games were in session. I swear there were a few who didn't stop playing cards once during the entire voyage.

The Colonel and one of the ship's officers arrived with a group of enlisted men carrying huge cartons. From these the Colonel drew what looked like a rubber belt about four inches wide. He passed one of these out to each girl, along with two cartridge-like affairs. The other men adjusted these to fit our waists, and they were certainly a bulky-looking arrangement. The cartridges screwed into one end of the belt, and you had only to give a sudden convulsive squeeze to explode them and so inflate the belt. Thereupon the slack, so to speak, which normally was folded over and snapped together, popped automatically open and the belt flew up under your armpits entirely inflated. Such a business! (Later, one of the girls inflated a major's life belt when he was becoming a bit out of hand on the blacked-out deck while they were star-gazing together.)

We found that troops were still being brought aboard and that it would probably be early morning before we would be ready to leave. Most of us wandered off in groups of two and three to watch the loading on of the troops with their backs bent low under the weight of the packs and shelter halves. I remember wondering, as we watched, whether any of them were our enlisted men, because up to then we had met none of the boys we were to work with through so many hardships later.

As we wandered around on A deck, lighted up by the glare of the floodlights that were being used to aid the stevedores, we came upon Kate and her Navy friend. They were just bringing out the victrola on deck and were enthusiastic about getting a group together to dance.

"You know, this is the last night we can have light of any kind out on deck," said the boy. "After we put to sea, the entire ship has to be blacked out, and I mean blacked out. You can't smoke from sundown to sunup, and all portholes must be closed at official sundown — which will be announced over the loud speaker daily. There will be only very dim lights in the lounge and foyer, and none at all in those places where there is no actual need of them. Did you know that the glow of a cigarette is supposed to be discernible for twelve miles at sea?"

"Oh bother with that kind of stuff," Kate said. "I want to dance." And with that she started to circle around deck humming to herself. She wasn't self-centered. She just knew what she wanted, and how to get it.

By this time several couples had arrived and were eagerly falling in with the idea of dancing. As I hadn't acquired an escort, I offered to wind the victrola. I sat there swinging my shoulders gently in time to the music when a pleasant, well-modulated voice at my elbow said:

"I believe you like to dance, too. Why not let someone else take a turn at winding this thing?"

I looked up to see a young man in his middle twenties who stood tapping his foot in rhythm with the record. He was just defying me to refuse his request to dance with him. So I laughed and stood up and stepped into his outstretched arms. We moved away as though we had always danced together, and he expressed surprise, as most young men do when they dance with me, that a girl of my size could dance so well!

After passing a pleasant evening, we were told that while we were on board ship we must be in our staterooms at eleven-forty-five and in bed for a twelve-o'clock check. We bade our newly found friends good night and retired to the stateroom, there to hold the usual "inquest" over the boys we had met and danced with that evening. Sometime during the next few minutes I decided I wanted to try sleeping in the upper bunk, and Kirk good-naturedly offered to trade with me for the night.

There was a small ladder-like affair which enabled one to get into the upper bunk with a little more ease. This had to be removed after getting into the bunk so that the girl below could get into hers. I managed to get my huge frame up onto the bunk amid much laughter from the girls, and then Kirk moved the ladder away.

Just then Miss Henry arrived and told us our lights must be out by twelve-fifteen. As she started to leave the stateroom she saw me peeking out between the bars of the bunk above and started to smile.

"I guess we have you now where we want you, haven't we? Are you in the doghouse, or are you up there from choice?"

"I thought it would be nice to see how the other half lives," I replied.

"Breakfast will be at seven o'clock, and we are to report to all meals. That's an order from the Colonel. So be sure you are there and on time!"

With this remark she flashed us a great big smile and left.

We had no sooner quieted down for the night than I felt the need for a cigarette and wished I had brought some to bed with me. Luckily, at about the same moment Kirk reached out to the bedside table, possessed of the same idea.

"Have you an extra one of those?" I whispered.

"Sure have, but not your brand."

"At this point," I said, "I'll smoke anything — even dried leaves." As I leaned down to get a light, I noticed she was crying.

"Would it help to talk about it," I asked, "or had you rather not?"

"Oh, I guess I'm just plain homesick," she sobbed. "We've stepped into a job that is going to be pretty big to handle. I'm going to miss my boy friend, too. Haskell, I guess I'm a big sissy!"

I wondered just how many of the girls were shedding a tear or two into their pillows in the darkness. Then suddenly I realized that most of these girls were mere children in their early twenties and taking their first big step by themselves. People expect men to be men, but they forget that women are not geared to the pace that war sets and that they have more difficulty in making their adjustments.

All too soon morning arrived, and I wakened to the excited sound of voices all talking at once.

"We are moving. What time is it?" asked Eleanor.

"Oh, look at the Statue of Liberty. Isn't it beautiful in the sunrise? I'll never forget this minute as long as I live," Marjie smiled, "Guess it's great to be an American. What do you think?"

"For goodness sakes move over and let me look," said little Millie, stepping up onto Eleanor's bed and trying to look out through a porthole already crowded with the other girls' heads.

"Hey, remember me? I want to see, too!" I shouted. I looked over the edge of the bunk and the floor seemed a long way down.

The girls were so excited, they forgot I was parked there in the second story, and not until we were well out into the harbor did I succeed in establishing my presence. I never did see the Statue of Liberty through a porthole!

We finally got ourselves dressed and to the mess hall; and when I perceived the look on the Colonel's face as one or two of the girls strolled in a few minutes late, I thought it was just as well I was among those who arrived on time.

"Girls, everybody is to report on deck for lifeboat drill sometime this morning, so be listening for the ship's whistle and then go directly to the lifeboat station that is assigned to you on the card in your stateroom. This is important, so try to be quiet and listen to what the CO. of Troops has to say to you. This is no picnic, and we are playing for keeps. I shall expect your fullest co-operation."

With this remark the Chief Nurse left us. Most of us wandered away to sit in the sun up on the boat deck. It seemed heavenly after the rush and hurly-burly of those last few days at camp, and at the Port of Embarkation, to have nothing to do but rest and relax in the sun.

Just about the time I got comfortable, the ship's whistle blew frantically and everybody seemed to know directly where they wanted to go, but it was such a mess to get there! I decided, then and there, I was going to push and shove just as much as anybody else, and I proceeded to elbow my way through to the companionway leading out to my boat station. I think at that point we stopped being meek and started working for what we wanted.

The CO. of Troops explained to us the whistle signals which called the crew to their battle stations and meant for all passengers to be on the alert, and the ones that were meant for all personnel to take their boat stations. He also told us we were always to come to boat drill wearing our helmets, life belts, and warm clothing. After he was well satisfied that we knew what was expected, he allowed us to go back to our staterooms.

Two or three days had passed without anything exciting happening when all of a sudden, just at lunch time, the ship's whistles gave the signal to take boat stations, and you should have seen those little colored waiters take to their heels and run. As we were running along the corridor, I noticed the grim expressions on the faces of the troops who were coming out of the hold of the ship to the decks to assume their posts at their boat stations. I hadn't thought much about it up to then, but I began to realize just how fortunate we girls were that we were allowed the freedom of the lounge and the decks while the enlisted personnel had no way of getting out into the air except at those appointed times when they were brought up on deck for their period of calisthenics. What had been something that they had not cared particularly for at camp now became a welcome thing as it enabled them to get outside and fill their lungs with good clean air after hours down below the level of the sea.

As we reached the deck on which we were to await the all clear signal, we found several officers at the rail gazing out to sea with their glasses.

"Would you like to look? That corvette over to the port side is firing at a submarine, see the splash of the water? That is the ash can exploding — I guess you call it a depth bomb." With this he handed me the glasses.

As I got them focused I saw a couple of corvettes, which are a little smaller than destroyers and very fast, chasing around in circles at the edge of the convoy firing off a depth bomb and dashing madly out of range of the thing as it exploded. This happened several times within the next twenty to twenty-five minutes. I noticed that, all the time, signals were being flashed from the bridge of various ships in the convoy.

Soon Mac, the officer whom we had met the first day on board, came by and told us that as far as could be learned they had made a hit on a submarine, for an oil slick and some wreckage were floating around in that vicinity. After what seemed like hours, the all clear sounded and we returned to the dining room. I think we were all a little subdued and frightened to realize just how near the subs could get to us, and also happy to see the efficient way that our escort boats went about taking care of the situation.

That evening after chow, just at blackout time, the sounds of piano music rose from the foyer, and everyone hesitated and then went down to B deck to see who was playing. We found a young officer from the signal corps outfit that was on board sitting at the piano, and although a goodly crowd began to gather, he apparently did not notice that there was anybody there. Soon those who had gathered around the piano began to hum, and the boy just modulated from one number into another with everybody singing. The bored, dissatisfied expression that had been prevalent on everybody's face changed to one of contentment, and I believe it was a good hour before anybody spoke a word, and then only to request that he play a favorite song. Somehow the spirit of friendliness that is transmitted through music is contagious, and as he swung into the strains of "Swing Low, Sweet Chariot," a beautiful bass voice entered into the melody. We all looked up the steps to discover the beaming face of the little colored waiter who worked at our table. Gradually everyone stopped singing and only hummed in snatches here and there, and that boy certainly could sing and tug at your heartstrings. The entire evening was spent in singing and listening to Lieutenant Glenn Davis play. Soon everyone retired for the night in a very mellow and satisfied mood. I could remember that as a child my mother and dad and brother and myself used to gather around the old organ and sing hymns, and it made me a little homesick for them again.

I was restless and uncomfortable trying to sleep in my slacks and sweater, but Miss Henry had emphasized the importance of sleeping in our clothes to us only that day, so my conscience would not allow me to take them off. We had to be ready at all times for the possible torpedoing of the ship, and we must not be where we would waste precious time in getting into our clothes. Still fussing to myself about the injustice of it all, I finally dropped off into a troubled sleep.

Clang, clang, clang! The sharp blast of the ship's whistle cut the air as we all struggled to get awake. There was the sound of hurrying feet over our head, and although I had been sleeping so soundly a moment before, I was suddenly very much awake.

"What time is it?" asked Kate.

"Four-thirty a.m. Surely it can't be practice drill at this ungodly hour. It must be the real McCoy. What do you think, Haskell?" asked Kirk as she swung her long legs down past my face in her scramble to get out of that upper bunk. (She didn't wait for the ladder either!)

"The Lord only knows, but we had better get ready to get out of here in a hurry," I said.

"I wish I knew whether this was real or not," said Millie. "Then I'd know whether to get excited or if it's just a waste of time getting all steamed up!"

As we talked, we had been getting into our overcoats, canteen belts, and life belts. We opened the door as we had been taught to do and stood there awaiting the order to proceed to the deck. We stood around and stood around, and about the time we decided we didn't care if the thing was real or not, we were told it was drill for the crew only and we could go back to bed. A fine thing!

About this time there was much discussion by everyone on board as to what our destination was to be. Some of the officers had been abroad in peacetime and they set themselves up as judges, although how anyone could judge a stretch of open sea is beyond me. The amusing thing was that none of them turned out to be right, in spite of their supposedly superior knowledge.

"I can't go to breakfast this morning. I don't feel well." With this Eleanor burrowed deeper into her pillow and promptly fell asleep again.

I cocked one eye open to see Millie standing at the washbasin trying to comb her hair, and every few minutes the ship would pitch so that she would have to hold to the side of the basin to keep her feet. She was decidedly pale; and the fact was, I was rapidly becoming very squeamish-feeling myself.

"Are you sick?" I asked as I tried to stand still long enough to get myself presentable.

"I could be very easily," Millie said, "but I'm going to try to get out on deck and see what happens."

"Wait a minute," I said, "and I'll go with you."

I splashed water hurriedly over my face, swept a comb through my hair, and we went up to mess. There were very few in the dining room, and we found it was raining very hard. Both of us struggled a cup of coffee down and decided we might as well be wet as sick, so we returned to our staterooms for our overcoats and went up on deck. The wind was howling, and the rain swept across the deck in sheets. As we held on to each other and worked our way up to the bow, many of the ship's officers whom we had become acquainted with in the days just past grinned their approval at our being out in the storm. Finally we reached a vantage point at the bow and stood there watching the other boats in the convoy tossing around as though they were bits of paper in a bathtub. The waves would break completely over the deck below, and we would get the full sweep of the spray in our faces. The sick feeling had long since passed, and there was something glorious in standing there facing the elements, braced against the wind, and the feel of the rain and spray in our faces. It made you feel good just to be alive and well. We stayed out on deck most of the morning and then returned to the stateroom to get into dry clothes before mess time.

"Where have you two lunatics been?" asked Eleanor.

"What makes you so wet?" Marjie wanted to know.

"Is it raining? How on earth did you manage to get up and get going? This old tub is bobbing around all over the place." With this remark Kate sat up for a second and promptly dropped back onto her cot.

"For goodness sakes," I said, "get these portholes open! No wonder you feel rotten. Yes, it's raining and has been for hours. Get up and go to mess and get outside, or you'll really be ill."

As Millie talked, she had been opening the ports and generally making a rumpus.

No amount of persuasion could drag the others out of their bunks, and we proceeded to get ready for mess.

As we entered the dining room, the little colored waiter grinned and told us he had seen us up on deck and that we were good sailors. (He should have seen me a couple of boat trips later!) There were only a few girls in the mess; and for that matter, not so many of the officers, either. I couldn't help but feel badly for the boys down in the hold, and I wondered how they were making out in such a confined space with the boat tossing as it was. One of the officers told us that we were hitting this bit of weather because we were getting up into the Irish Sea (though I still don't see why everything disagreeable has to be blamed on the Irish!). The day finally passed, and along toward night the sea became more calm. The nurses and officers were nearly all present for the evening meal. Millie and I were particularly proud that we had managed to stay on our feet the entire day in spite of the way we felt when we had awakened that morning.

The day dawned bright and clear after the storm of yesterday. As we stood at the rail watching a school of porpoises. Miss Henry arrived and told us all that we had about two hours to pack, that some of us were to be put ashore at one port and the rest of the personnel at another. What had looked to be a cloud in the distance turned out to be land! We were amazed we hadn't realized what it was.

We returned to our stateroom to get our things together and were much excited to realize that our voyage was nearly over, and without any serious mishaps.

"I wonder where we are?" I asked.

"Could be most anywhere in the British Isles, from the route we have been following," answered Marjie.

We smiled to ourselves, for since Marjie had been tagging around with the navigation officer on board, she had become worldly wise in the whys and wherefores of life at sea.

"Anyway, we won't be in doubt much longer, will we?" answered Kirk.

"I don't really care," said Eleanor, "just as long as I set foot on dry land once again. I've had all the sea voyage I want for some time to come!" With this remark she slammed her suitcase shut and sat on it so she could lock the thing.

"Fall in!" boomed the voice of the Colonel in the corridor.

We stepped out of our rooms and into the corridor still trying to get all our belongings together.

"This is it! We are about to step our feet onto foreign soil. Do not make any audible remarks about the people, their appearance, or their country. They are as rightly proud of their home as we are of ours, and we must not forget even for a minute that we are ambassadors of good will from our country to the ones we shall have to live in. Be kind and pleasant, and above all be courteous! I shall personally see that anyone that is discourteous or sneering about anything or anybody shall be punished. You will march down the gangplank directly along the dock and into the train standing at the extreme end. March in from the back of the cars and fill the seats as you come to them. Do not argue about trivial things. The impressions that we make from here on in are important in determining the attitude these people will take toward us. I know you won't fail me!"

The Colonel smiled and walked rapidly to the head of the line.

"Attention! Forward march!"

As we walked along the companionway, the expressions on the faces of the officers who were watching us were something to see. Many fast friendships had been formed in a very short while, and it was running through everyone's mind that we might not ever see each other again. It was not without regret that we left what had been our home for the past few days.

Down the gangplank and onto the dock! Scotland! Will you like us?

CHAPTER THREE An Introduction to Another Land

"Hut, two, three, four, hut, two, three, four," boomed the voice of Lieutenant William Wheeler, who had been placed temporarily in charge of the nurses.

We marched along in a soldierly manner, looking neither to right nor left, although I must confess we were all nearly dying with curiosity. Two by two we filed into the train that was waiting for us, and you can imagine our surprise when we discovered that instead of an aisle going down the middle of each car — as at home — there was an aisle down the left side onto which opened a series of compartments with seats facing each other and comfortably seating six. So, true to the Army way of doing things, we had eight in each compartment! As we got into our places and removed our gas masks and musette bags and began to breathe once again, we crowded around the windows to see what sort of country we were in.

Everything seemed to be so spotlessly clean. The workers in the railway yards were all women, dressed in dungarees like the men in our own yards at home. This seemed very strange to us because, as yet, women had not begun to do that kind of work in the States.

"Bless her heart, just look at her!" exclaimed Marjie with a catch in her voice.

"Who, where?" asked Eleanor.

"Out there on my side of the train. She's about the most precious thing I've seen in some time. Have a look!"

We crowded over to investigate the cause of so much admiration, and there, at the side of the train, stood a young mother of about eighteen with a tiny infant in her arms. Both mother and child made the V sign for victory — a sight which brought a very large lump to my throat. Their faces were cleanly scrubbed, but it was evident that their clothing had been patched and repatched until it was no longer possible to say for sure what the original materials had been.

"She looks like your Carl might have looked at that age," remarked Marjie.

"Yes," I said, "she certainly does. But thank goodness, my Carl is growing up in a country that is untouched by the ravages of war. And God willing, let us hope it remains that way, too!"

"Would you young ladies like something to eat?" asked a kindly voice over our shoulders.

We turned away from the window and the baby to see a wholesome looking girl standing there in our compartment with a huge basket of what appeared to be flapjacks.

"We sure would!" I replied. And with that we each reached into the basket and drew one of them out.

"They really haven't any name," the girl explained. "But they are right filling, and maybe you will like them. You know, young ladies, we people of Scotland are very happy that the Yanks have arrived. We know you are here to help us, and we need that help badly. My man has been gone two years now. I expect he wouldn't know our baby."

She passed along to the next compartment, and we sat there munching in silence. Several other women came to the compartment door and gave us cookies which they called cakes. Also hot buns and jelly.

"I understand food is rationed over here," I said, stopping one of the younger ones. "Don't you people need these things you're giving away?"

She leaned over, smiled, and said, "Please don't worry about us. We couldn't have you thinking you weren't going to like your new country. So we ladies put our flour together, and a few other things we fancied you might care for."

"Are you Scottish?" asked Kate with an abruptness that sounded almost impudent.

The girl shook her blonde head. "My husband is. He's in the Scottish Army, and I'm living with his parents."

"Husband?" Kate gasped. "You old enough to have a husband?"

"Why, I'm seventeen. And what's more, I have two fine babies. We're going to America after it's all over," she added proudly.

I thought to myself: Seventeen, and twice a mother, and her husband out there fighting somewhere. And yet she carries on as though nothing were happening. Secretly I was beginning to have a great deal of respect for these people who could take so much punishment and not even whimper about it.

At this point Colonel Ringer poked his head into the compartment and beamed a smile at us. "Everything all right with you girls?" he asked casually.

"Couldn't be better," I said, speaking for my companions. "Do you know where we're going?"

"That, my dear, is a question you can answer as well as I can!" He winked and then stalked off down the car to check on the rest of his charges.

The Scottish women left the train now and stood around on the platform chatting with us through the windows. They seemed so sincere, so very friendly, that we rather felt lost as the train started to move away without them.

"Look at the houses," Eleanor said a few moments later as we proceeded slowly through the town. "Aren't they tiny?"

"Yes, but what adorable gardens," put in Kate. "And the grass. It's so green — so well kept."

It was true that each house had its fenced-off yard and flower garden, no matter how small. The fences were made of rock which had doubtless to be carried in from the fields beyond the town.

We passed a convent school. There were many little children in the enclosure, from five to ten or twelve years of age. All of them pressed up close to the fence to watch us pass.

"I think we really are welcome here, kids," I said to my companions in the compartment. "Just look at those youngsters. Even they seem glad to see us."

Every last one of them was making a V for victory. It seemed to be both a promise and a prayer!

The fields were ablaze with red poppies now, and coming around a curve we caught a glimpse of the sea in the distance. Then Colonel Ringer and the Chief Nurse arrived with word that we would no doubt be on the train the entire night and should make ourselves as comfortable as possible with our overcoats for warmth.

"Remember, girls," cautioned the Colonel, "we are now in a country where absolute blackout must be observed. Don't smoke without being certain that the shades are drawn and properly fastened. We'd not have much of a chance if the train were bombed, and we haven't even started the job that we came to perform. So don't get careless."

It was August in Scotland. Soon the sky began to take on the most exquisite colors, and at the same time one could almost feel the temperature changing. From the friendly warmth of a few minutes ago, it was suddenly cold and damp. We began to be glad we were sitting eight in a compartment, as we derived some degree of warmth from the contact of each other's bodies. We were all huddled up together, some alert and homesick, and others dozing as though they didn't have a care in the world, when one of the medical officers opened the door and told us to get our canteen cups ready as we were to stop a few miles up the line for a hot drink. This suggestion was most welcome indeed, and we began messing around our equipment to get at them. As usual, they were on the bottom of the pile.

We were amazed to learn that we got off the train on the side away from the aisle — a sort of one-way-street arrangement. You got on at one side and off at the other.

The train rolled to a stop under a shed-like affair, and there stood women in some sort of uniform which we learned was the Home Defense uniform, and before them were two large cauldrons of hot beverage. I don't know to this day what it was we were drinking, but I do know it was the only thing that stood between me and death by freezing.

"You may walk a bit," said Miss Henry. "But don't wander away, for these trains give no warning when they start up again. They just start, and if you are left, it's too bad."

This was a welcome order, for we were stiff and cramped from riding sardine-can fashion. Soon we were back in our compartment again, and the train started on its way. As we were pulling out of the shed, the sound of bagpipes became pleasantly audible, and we crowded around the window to see a group of six men in kilties marching along and serenading us.

Nightfall in a strange new land. We were pretty much excited and a little frightened. We were in a country where bombs were more than just talk, and I guess we were secretly apprehensive about what the future might bring. Finally we dozed off to sleep in the most grotesque positions possible, and my last conscious thought was: Oh, Lord, I'll never be the same woman again!

I woke up to see Kirk wiggling her five-feet-nine-inches around, doubtless checking to determine whether she were still in one piece.

"Good morning," I said sweetly.

"Don't mention it," came the sleepy reply.

The door of the compartment was suddenly pushed open and Louise Miller stood there smiling at us. "Do you girls know we are in England?" she whispered, out of consideration to the others who somehow managed to be sleeping. "We came through London about six o'clock this morning. The sunrise was beautiful. You should have seen it.

Now, it seemed, everyone in the compartment was awake and wondering what England would be like.

We rode another two or three hours and finally arrived at some little town tucked away down in southern England. As we had had nothing to eat since the evening before, when the Scottish ladies had so generously fed us, we were becoming very much interested in whether or not we were to have breakfast. No one seemed to know much about that particular thing, and we were finally loaded onto buses for the completion of the trip. We were wearing gas masks, canteen belts and canteens, and a musette bag, not exactly conducive to being comfortable when sitting two in a seat on a crowded bus. Kate Rodgers was my seatmate, and between her and myself and all our equipment there wasn't any room to spare.

"How long do we have to ride, do you know?" asked Louise Miller.

"I don't think very long, from what the Colonel said," replied Miss Henry. "I hope not, anyway, as this pack is getting mighty uncomfortable and I'm hungry!"

After we had ridden about an hour, the buses suddenly stopped. We just sat there until everyone was ready to scream, and when we could stand it no longer, one of the girls asked the driver what we were stopped for. He informed us we were waiting for the Colonel to eat his breakfast. Now, you may have seen disturbed people before, but the expressions on those girls' faces was something to behold. I guess at that point we all wished we had a silver leaf on our shoulders!

Soon we started off again, and by this time everyone's nerves were on edge and we were so tired we could have slept in the street.

"Haskell, catch her, quick!" yelled Doris Brittingham.

I looked up with a start, as I had been riding with my eyes closed, just in time to see Kate fall off the seat into the aisle, field equipment and all. She had fallen asleep and gotten off balance as we rounded a curve. She woke up in a hurry, much disgruntled about the whole thing and a little peeved because we had laughed at her.

Soon we came to what seemed to be a good-sized town. As we started through it, the driver slowed down and said,

"You girls missed the excitement. There was a bombing here last night. Jerry came over and left his calling card."

Directly ahead of us traffic was being routed around a lot of debris in the street, and several houses in the section had great, gaping holes in their roofs and side walls. We could look into one of them, and a woman was standing at the kitchen stove cooking the noonday meal.

"Was anybody injured?" several of us asked at once.

"I really don't know," the bus driver said. "But I imagine so, as it happened in the dead of night."

"What are those things?" I asked, pointing to what appeared to be several Zeppelin-like affairs in the sky.

"Barrage balloons," answered the driver. "They are over all the possible targets in this town. There is a large cable attached to them, and they can be raised or lowered at will. Planes can't get in low enough to dive-bomb without becoming entangled in the cables, and by that time our anti-aircraft can let them have it," he replied.

"If that is the case, what about this bombing last night?" asked one of the girls.

"Jerry outsmarted us. Came in from the side of town away from the balloons. Evidently a 'recon' plane had been over in the daytime and learned the way around."

"What a beautiful church!" exclaimed Miss Henry.

"Yes," replied the driver, and you could almost see him swell with pride. "That church is one of the oldest in England and one of the richest in tradition. You must attend services there. It will do your very soul good just to walk through there."

All this time we had been riding through what was a very pretty English town, and now we were climbing a long hill. As we reached the top, the driver swung the bus through a gate at which an American soldier stood on guard — and didn't he look good to us!

"Well, girls, here you are," said the driver. "Guess you won't be sorry to get out, will you?"

With that remark he drove up before the steps of a long barracks-like building and stopped. As he stopped the bus and got out to help us down, an American major and three nurses came down the steps of the building.

"Welcome home, girls," said one of the nurses. "Come in and make yourselves comfortable. You look exhausted. I'm Miss Wilbur." She led us up the steps into the large recreation room of the building.

I was struggling with the straps of my pack when the major said,

"You seem to be having trouble. May I help you?" And he proceeded to get me out of my equipment.

"If you will come over to the barracks, we will assign rooms to you girls, and then we will take you to the mess hall to eat!"

Food! After all those hours on the train and bus we were actually going to eat once again. Our spirits began to revive just at the thought of it.

"Come this way, girls," said the nurse. "This barracks over here is empty. Fall in and go directly to the back of the building, and fill the rooms as you come to them, two girls to a room."

She threw open the door, and we all trailed in. Beds! Real beds with inner-spring mattresses, and showers. Such luxury, and everything so spotlessly clean. Soon what had been a tired, disgruntled group of women was transformed into a giggling group of girls ready to indulge in a little horseplay.

"Great day in the morning! This is a beautiful war," said Vaughn Fisher, one of the girls from the Fort Knox group.

"It certainly is," agreed her roommate, Virginia Ayers. "I think when I'm fed I'll be ready to live once again."

"Eats! Let's hurry over to the mess hall. Miss Wilbur said they were waiting dinner for us, and I for one can really do justice to a little nourishment!" I replied.

Soon we had attained that comfortable feeling one gets after filling an empty stomach. We wandered back to our barracks in a leisurely manner, no one having a great deal to say.

"After you girls have rested a bit, there will be a meeting in the recreation hall where you came in. Major Humphries has a few things he wants to say to you. We will let you know the exact time." It was Miss Wilbur speaking.

We went to our rooms and curled up on our beds to sleep for a bit, for we had got very little rest on that train the night before. My aching muscles certainly did like the feel of the luxury of that bed. Just as I was dozing off, a young voice with a very decided British accent said:

"Pardon me, lady, I'm Ivy. Here are some clean towels for you and an extra cover for your bed." She smiled at me, then added: "You know, it gets very cold in this country after nightfall. Do you know how to close your blackout screens? That is very important over here, you know. Jerry came over last night, and we don't want to break the blackout here, for there are many sick people about who could not help themselves."

Thereupon she stepped up onto a chair to show me how to adjust the curtain. Such a tiny little girl she appeared to be. As she stepped down again, I saw her looking longingly at a package of cigarettes that I had carelessly thrown upon the dresser.

"Would you like one?" I asked, handing her the pack.

"Oh, I certainly would, miss. It's been a long time since I have had an American cigarette of any kind, and we like them better than we do our own!"

Ivy was to prove herself valuable to us through the next few weeks. She gave us directions on how to get to church and where the best shops were, and she even took my shoes to the cobbler's after several hours of road marches and close-order drill had worn the bottoms out of them.

Soon we gathered in the recreation hall to listen to what the good Major might have to say to us.

"Well," he began, "I must say you are a different-looking group of young ladies than the ones who arrived here a few hours ago. I guess a little soap and water, good food, and rest were what the doctor ordered!" He smiled, and somehow one felt instantly at ease. Then he resumed his serious expression and continued:

"As you know, we are only across the Channel from where all hell is breaking loose. Once in a while Jerry gets around to flying over us. Many times nothing happens, and then again he may drop a calling card as he did last night. I, personally, have been bombed, and I go on record as saying it isn't a pleasant experience. Remember, therefore, that blackout is important and must not be broken. It is not only your own life you fool with when you are careless but the lives of hundreds around you."

When the Major had established his point. Miss Wilbur took the floor and explained about air raids. "There are warning signals on each ramp connecting these barracks," said she. "When you hear the signal, you are to stay in your rooms unless directly ordered to proceed to the shelters. Remember, if you do go to the shelters, not to sit with your backs to the wall. Lean away from the wall with your elbows on your knees. If you are caught out of doors when a plane comes over, drop to the ground and lie still. A running figure attracts attention. Do not look up. The reflection of light from your face can be seen for several thousand feet. If Jerry starts dropping them around you, lift your body off the ground with your elbows and hold your mouth open. And right now, don't look so frightened. I've been here a year, and I'm still hale and hearty!"

When Miss Wilbur finished speaking, we retired to our rooms to rest so that we might have energy enough to explore the town next day. It seemed we were not to be assigned to work for a few days at least. We needed time in which to get our land legs back again. The weather was exceptionally cold, and we were grateful for the extra cover that Ivy had given us.

Next day, in town, I learned about money. I didn't know I could be so dumb! It seemed to me that I handed over perfectly good American money and received a handful of wallpaper in exchange. And the pennies! They were as big as our half dollars. A shilling was approximately twenty-four cents and a sixpence was worth about a dime. A ten-shilling note was two dollars, and a pound was four dollars and eight cents. The worst of it was, we began to spend pound notes as promiscuously as though they were dollar bills! Arithmetic never was my forte, and this rate of exchange was too much for me.

The town was so different from anything I had ever seen that it intrigued me. Nearly everything was rationed, so all we could do was window-shop. The stationers (or bookstores) were intensely interesting to me, and I browsed around for hours by myself before we left. It seemed strange to see the sign "Chemist Shop" over a drugstore. And everyone stood in line at the bus stops before a sign reading "Queue up here for bus." And the buses themselves were double-decker affairs with women drivers and women collecting the fares. (They certainly did an efficient job of it, though.) The good old familiar red front of an F. W. Woolworth store loomed up on the next corner, but instead of the usual five-and-ten-cent sign over the door it said three and six. Threepence for five cents and a sixpence for a dime! My head was in a whirl and I vowed I'd never be able to figure it out, though amazingly enough I did, and in a rather short time.

As we walked along, talking eagerly and seeing everything for the first time, we noticed that all the English women, young and old, were looking at us as though we were something to behold. We couldn't understand it, and finally, as we were standing before a shop window, I asked a kindly-appearing woman in her middle forties,

"Please, ma'am, what is wrong with us? Why do you all look at us so strangely?"

She laughed a little self-consciously and replied,

"It's your legs, ma'am. You all have such pretty legs and feet, and those silk stockings that you are wearing are the most beautiful things we have seen over here in three years! You know, there hasn't a woman gone by you who hasn't envied you your stockings! It's been so long since we have had them!"

I thanked her for telling us, and we passed on, a little subdued that something that we took for granted could be the source of so much attention from a people grown accustomed to going without so many things.

Next we went into a shop and asked if we could buy anything to eat or drink. The salesgirl looked at us as though we were demented.

"Lor' no, not until after four o'clock," she said. "Of course we can give you tea then."

I'd always heard about four o'clock tea, and I gave a standing vote of one that we stay for it. As it was now three-forty, the others agreed we might as well stay and see what it was all about.

We wandered down the street to pass the time and came onto the most weird-looking store front I had ever seen. Up over the door on a very crooked sign was the caption, "House of Crooked Steps." And a little white card, in the none-too-clean window, read, "Tea and cakes, 4 P.M." It intrigued us so, we went in and sat down.

These English certainly believed in tradition and in doing things the way they have done them for generations. Four o'clock was the hour for tea; and although we sat there for fully fifteen minutes, I swear the rather bored-looking waitress did not come over to take our order until the old grandfather's clock, standing in the corner, had struck four. We found that you paid threepence for a cup of tea (without sugar), and tuppence each for little cakes and paper-thin cucumber sandwiches. It was fun and certainly different from any lunch we had ever bought in the States. Soon we were headed back up the long hill to where we were staying.

"Look," said Kate, "everybody seems to be riding bicycles, even the older women. I'd like to ride one, too."

We had done quite a lot of riding while stationed at Camp Forrest, for the post exchange used to have them to rent. So we decided to look around with a view to carrying out Kate's idea.

After looking in vain for a bicycle shop, I remembered there were some bicycles at the warehouse that some of the girls had left who had been transferred to other stations, and that we might ride them if we wanted to. As it was getting late, we made our plans for the following afternoon.

The day was bright and sunny, and we decided to go out the country road just below our barracks and see what the countryside was like. Besides, we were wearing slacks and sweaters, and we didn't know how the general public would take to our tearing around town in pants.

Everything went fine until we started down a long hill and tried to back-pedal and brake the darn things. Nothing happened! The farther we went the faster we went, and we couldn't slow down. To make matters worse, a farmer with an ox team was crossing the road just at the bottom of the hill. Luckily I discovered in the nick of time that, instead of being coaster-braked like our American bicycles, these had brakes on the handle bars, so that all one had to do was to compress them gently to slow down and stop. I yelled to the girls, they caught on immediately, and we came to a safe stop a few yards short of the farmer and his team.

We rode leisurely home, only to arrive upon a scene of activity. It seemed that the Colonel had been there and decided we should be kept busy. So we were to start the next morning at seven with calisthenics, with classes for several hours a day. I expect he was right, but just at that minute I didn't like the idea at all. There were so many places I wanted to go and so much I wanted to see. But in the Army one does as the Army wishes.

It took us several weeks to become accustomed to the English people and their way of doing things. Then one day the Colonel burst the bombshell that we were to join the rest of the outfit in tents!

Accordingly we packed up and were taken by truck convoy to the English military reservation about twenty miles away. We found we were not to go into tents but rather into the cylinder-like metal affairs known as Miesen huts. Ten girls to a hut. The enlisted men in our outfit had been sent to get the huts in readiness for us, and they had made the beds. We should have been suspicious, but somehow we were a trusting lot. When we got ready to go to bed that night every last cot for sixty girls had been made up short-sheeted! We started to get in, tired enough to drop, only to discover that our feet went down no farther than about two feet. Most of us could see the joke, but the others got out of bed and did considerable grumbling while fixing their beds so that they might sleep in them.

I wondered then what kind of field soldiers we were going to make.

CHAPTER FOUR Life in an English Military Reservation

We were awakened by the shrill blast from the Sergeant's whistle and the heavy boom of a male voice saying:

"Come on now, everybody out. Calisthenics this morning. Let's get this show on the road! Front and center on the double!"

With a low moan and a groan we stumbled out of bed, ran our hands through our tumbled hair, and stepped out into the chill, damp cold of an English morning. The dew was heavy and glistening in the light of the slowly rising sun. It didn't seem possible it was only early fall.

"Fall in!" barked our tormentor. "I think you have already been told you nurses are to undergo a drill and training period while here at this reservation. You will report each morning for exercise at seven o'clock sharp. This will last for twenty minutes. Breakfast at seven-thirty, and then you will return to put your barracks in order. Classes will start promptly at eight-thirty, and you will have two hours of close-order drill from nine-thirty to eleven-thirty. Lunch is from twelve to one, and classes from one to five. No one will be excused, and we expect you to be prompt."

With these words, he finished speaking, and we were then put through the stiffest twenty minutes of exercise I had ever taken in my life. Some of it wasn't so bad, but the jumping exercises wrecked the dignity of some of the heavy-chested girls. Especially Louise Miller and myself.

"I think," said little, demure Ann Boyd, "this business is a lot of nonsense! I came over here to take care of sick men, not to be made a soldier! I don't think it is right to expect us to do all this strenuous work."

"I guess they want to toughen us up for whatever it is that's ahead of us," remarked Whitey, a pal of Boyd's from Fort Knox. "You must admit we are pretty soft — look at us!"

We glanced around, and it was really laughable to see the various girls rubbing aching muscles here and there, with weird expressions on their faces. Some of us had used muscles in that last twenty minutes that we hadn't even thought of since we so painstakingly learned about them in training days.

"I'm hungry," said Ginny Ayers. "Let's hurry up with this cleaning-up business and go to chow!"

"I haven't washed yet, wait for me," said Doris Friedlund as she picked up the pail and started across the company street to the combination shower room and latrine.

Such a funny sort of place to make one's toilet. In the center of the room was a trough-like affair with about half a dozen spigots running above it. A central shelf ran along about two and a half feet over the trough on which you could park your toilet things. We lined up, six girls to a side, and washed our faces and cleaned our teeth. There was no happy medium in the water situation. It was either too hot or too cold. One time you shivered so hard it wasn't necessary to dry your face, and the next time you couldn't hold the face cloth under the spigot long enough to get it wet!

Soon we joined the others in the mess hut and thoroughly enjoyed our breakfasts. Especially cup after cup of hot coffee. That seems to be the mainstay of the breakfast, in this man's army. We then spent an hour at class and reported to the open area at the rear of kitchen huts for the drill period. It developed that Captain Forman and Sergeant Roberts were going to be our drillmasters. Captain Forman explained to us the various movements we were to execute and then separated us into two groups, he taking one of them and Sergeant Roberts the other. I swear I didn't know there were so many people with two left feet and no sense of rhythm. A couple of those girls couldn't even march! The situation wasn't helped in the least by the grins on the faces of the enlisted men who were watching us from the sidelines. I supposed it amused them to see a group of girls make such a mess of the orders that were just second nature to them. After a fashion we struggled through and then were dismissed.

When I arrived back at the hut, the girls were prone on their cots resting for the few minutes before chow time. I didn't enter into the conversation at first as I wanted to look around and learn a little about my hut-mates. On each move we were assigned to a different group, and I seemed to be the only one in this particular group who wasn't with some mutual friend. Two of the girls were from Camp Wheeler in Georgia, seven of them were from Fort Knox, and I was the only one from Camp Forrest. Just about the time we were nicely relaxed. Lieutenant Salter, who had recently been appointed assistant to the chief nurse, stuck her head in the door and told us it was chow time.

We started up the company street toward the mess tent when Lieutenant Salter said:

"How many of you would like to go dancing tonight? The officers of the infantry outfit a few miles from here want to have a party. They called Colonel Ringer, and he said we might go but that we must be back on the area at eleven-thirty. They will send a truck for us. How about it?"

There were crys of "Count me in," "Sure, we all want to go," and "Are the officers nice, or old, baldheaded, and fifty-five?"

Finally Lieutenant Salter laughed and held up her hands in despair.

"There will be a notice posted in my hut. If you want to go to the party, come in and sign your names to it and be ready to leave at seven o'clock."

We chatted gaily as we continued along our way to chow. It's amazing what the thought of a little music and he company of nice young men can do to the morale of a group of tired girls!

The afternoon finally wore away, and as we left each lecture period I couldn't decide whether it would be my final fate to be bombed, to die from snake bite, to have either malaria or dysentery, or to be gassed. I swear each lecture course made you just a little bit more confused about all the possible things that might happen to you. At least there was never a dull moment.

Gone were the days when a gal went modestly into the shower in a robe and pulled a curtain protectingly across while she scrubbed herself. After the supper meal those who were going to the party tore across the road and undressed in the cold of that unheated building, piled clothes on the floor, and ducked under the shower at once. As we stood around and washed each other's back, the conversation ran like this:

"I hope I meet somebody nice at that party. This being engaged is all right, but not very satisfactory when you are in one country and he is in another."

"I sure hope that whoever takes me in tow can dance," I said, shaking the water out of one ear. "I'd rather dance than eat, and you kids know how I like to eat."

"I won't believe it until I see it," said Mary Meyer.

"Believe what?" asked Marjie, who was already applying the towel across her middle.

"I won't believe there's an officer in this man's army who isn't married and hasn't at least two children. And I don't cotton to married men."

"What the heck," piped up Ginny Ayers. "We aren't planning on marrying any of them."

Seven o'clock finally arrived, and right on the dot a couple of army trucks rolled up before the barracks. We were ready and waiting, our make-up correct, and each wearing her favorite perfume. (Wooing water, as one of the girls so aptly called it.) One cannot be very glamorous in a G.I. uniform, but then it isn't how one looks so much as how one behaves that's important. We were boosted into the trucks by the few officers who came along as a sort of reception committee, and if the rest of them were to be as nice, I could see the makings of a large evening.

Eventually we rolled into the drive of a three-story brick building. It was beautiful, with English ivy completely covering the façade.

We found our hosts to be officers of an infantry regiment. They were a fine group of men and gave us a beautiful evening. The main hall had been converted into a bar of sorts, at which one could get some thoroughly atrocious Irish whiskey, some rather good Burgundy, lemon pop, and ginger ale. On one side of this hall was a large room in which the orchestra was playing, and on the other side a room of equal dimensions with a fireplace at either end and huge lounge chairs all about. This made us a little envious, because our only chair was a packing box and our only fire came from a little bucket-type stove in which nothing, for any length of time, could be prevailed upon to burn.

Eleven-thirty came entirely too soon, and we were taken out to the trucks, packed in, and carted back to our base. The boys were in a very happy mood as we left them and were certain they would have us back again. Of course they never did. Wars don't seem to wait upon the pleasure of those who take part in them!

Morning again, and that blasted whistle. Out we went and lined up promptly, for we felt that the sooner we got into line, the sooner would we be through. At the order for us to bend over and touch our toes, the groan that arose could have been heard by Hitler in Berchtesgaden. Lieutenant Katzowitz was giving us our workout that morning, and he surely didn't spare the horses. I guess it was what we needed to iron out the kinks we had acquired the day before, but it wasn't too easy to take. Somehow we lived through the whole twenty minutes, but I think that the grin on Katz's face was the most malicious I've ever seen!

The next couple of days passed much as though we had always been at this basic training, and it was amazing to see the color come into the cheeks of the girls and the bright, clear sparkle in their eyes. And appetites! We were all eating as we had never eaten before. I guess the out-of-door exercise was really agreeing with us, and our muscles were really responding to calisthenics. We weren't doing so badly at drill, either, and some of us almost enjoyed it.

"Have you seen the bulletin board?" asked Whitey one morning after chow. "We're to go on a road march this afternoon for a two-hour period. We're to wear canteen belts, have our canteens full of water, and carry our gas masks. Also we're to wear our helmets and G.I. shoes. Captain Markham is to take us. Now how do you like that?"

"Personally, I don't think so much of it," announced Helen English, who had come through the door while Whitey was speaking.

Just then there was the screech of the air-raid whistle on top of the headquarters building of the engineers encamped just below us. This bloodcurdling sound was soon joined by the wail of the siren from the field artillery group far away on the next hill. We watched from the window, and it was startling to see how quickly the area was cleared. Where there had been many soldiers milling around a second before, there was no one but the guard walking his post and scanning the heavens. Soon a squadron of British planes passed overhead, and the drone of their motors was indeed good to hear. Shortly the all clear sounded, and everything dropped back into a routine once again. I didn't so much mind the air-raid warnings in the day time, but there was something very terrifying about them in the dead of night.

"I wonder where we are going and how fast a cadence he will set?" asked Helen.

"Probably won't be too fast," replied Doris Friedlund. "He's kind of fat, and I imagine he'll like to take it easy too!"

"Guess we had better get going if we're to be up at headquarters by one-thirty. The Colonel is going to inspect us, so we'd better be there and ready when he comes by," Ann replied.

It was a heavenly afternoon and just the kind of day to be outside. As we were standing there at ease, the Colonel arrived, called us to attention, and said:

"You girls must begin to get toughened to this sort of thing. From the information in my possession, I feel that your physical stamina must be strengthened considerably. Captain Markham is to take you on this road march. No one is to drop out unless she can't possibly make it, and I expect you to perform in a military manner and execute your orders with military precision."

Just then Captain Markham arrived, a little flustered that the CO. had got there ahead of him.

"Attention! Forward march! Hut, two, three, four, hut, two, three, four. Dress it up there, and you on the ends, cover!"

He was really putting it to us, and as we had to go up a hill in whatever direction he chose to take us, we all prayed that he would either cut the cadence or give us route step. This meant that instead of marching we could walk along at the rate most comfortable, as long as we didn't break ranks and kept some semblance of being in formation. Soon we swung through the gate and out onto the macadam road. As we turned a column left and started off down toward the engineers' area, a group of troops on march passed us, and the low, underlying whistle that is always present when a soldier sees a girl was heard. Soon we passed out of sight of the camp, and Captain Markham grinned and shouted,

"Route step, march! I didn't want this job, but as long as I seem to have had it wished on me, where would you like to go?"

"Home, if you don't mind," sounded an unidentified voice from the rear.

With that we all broke into a laugh. We were walking along at not-too-leisurely a rate, when I began to be conscious that my feet were hurting. I have a rather small foot, and the only pair of G.I. shoes they could find for me at the time was two and a half sizes too large; and no matter how many pair of hose I donned, they just sailed around on my feet like gunboats. Our shoes were exactly what the enlisted men wear in the field. As we walked farther along, I was really in agony and began to limp. Soon I noticed some of the other girls were limping, too.

"Captain Markham, sir. How about a ten-minute break?" asked Vaughn Fisher. "I am sure my feet are blistered!"

"Wait until we get over the brow of the hill, over into that wooded area where there will be some shade. Then we'll have a few minutes of rest," answered the Captain. I noticed there was considerable perspiration on his upper lip, too.

"Company halt!" he barked at last. "Dismissed!"

With a sigh we dropped down upon a bed of pine needles, and for a minute a terrific wave of homesickness washed over me. The last time I had sat on pine needles had been in Maine.

As soon as we were seated, I unlaced my shoes and took my socks off, and sure enough there were two whopping big blisters on each foot, and me with about two miles to walk back to camp. I pulled my socks back on and sat there with my back against a tree resting, and I guess I must have fallen asleep, because the next thing I knew the Captain was shouting:

"Attention! Fall in!"

I struggled hastily to my feet, only to discover I didn't have my shoes on. Everyone else was in formation, and there I sat at the foot of that tree putting my shoes on. Needless to say, my face was very red.

"At ease, girls. It seems the duchess has to have a little time to make her toilet!" This in the good Captain's most sarcastic manner.

"Lieutenant Haskell, would it inconvenience you too much to fall in now?" snapped he a moment later, sounding definitely irritated.

"Yes, sir!" I replied and hastily took my place in the ranks, feeling like Doghouse Annie.

By the time we swung in through the gates at camp I could hardly walk, and several others were having the same difficulty. As we marched up in front of headquarters to be dismissed, we were a sorry-looking lot. It had been hot in the afternoon sun, and that, along with the discomfort of feet blistering, bad really been something.

The Colonel came out, took one look, and said, "There, girls, do you see what I mean? You have to get used to doing this, for we don't know when the time will come when we'll have to depend on our feet for our very safety."

I prayed for a second that somebody would dismiss us soon, because I wanted to cry, my feet were hurting me so. I swear I don't blame the enlisted men for dropping out when their company is on road march if they get as uncomfortable as I was.

"Any of you who have blisters on your feet," said the Captain, "report for sick call in the morning. Dismissed."

With that command we broke ranks and started for our barracks a good distance from where we were. I staggered in and sat down on my cot. Little Ginny Ayers came over and unlaced my shoes and took them off, and for a minute I thought I couldn't stand the wave of pain that passed through my feet when the pressure of the shoes was removed. When I took my socks off, both feet were bleeding. Over on the other side of the room Ann Boyd and Whitey were in the same fix. I pitied them from the bottom of my heart, because I knew how I felt.

In a couple of days I felt much better, although I still walked rather gingerly. The week end was coming up, and we heard we were going to get passes to go into London. London! One of the places I had always dreamed of but really never expected to see. I went immediately to headquarters and asked for a pass, and it was granted. I knew there would be so many wanting to go that only the first requests would be granted, because we were only allowed to have ten per cent of the command away from the area at any one time. Marjie Hart, Millie Harris, and myself decided to go together as we had been given passes and we didn't know when we would all get to go on a spree again.

Finally Saturday afternoon rolled around, and we left camp by bus for the station. We learned it was about a two-hour run into London.

"Miss Salter told me we must stay at the American Red Cross Nurses' Club at Grosvenor Square so in case they need us they will know where to reach us," volunteered Millie.

"Just think where we are going," exclaimed Marjie.

"London! I've always wanted to see Buckingham Palace and Hyde Park, and ever so many places I have read about for years."

At the station we learned that the fare was about three dollars, American money. It seemed strange that you didn't buy a ticket and then give it to someone on the train, as we do at home. Instead you gave it to a man who stood outside closed gates. When it was time for the train, he allowed you to go through the gates, and only those who had tickets could be admitted. Soon the funny little old train steamed in, and there followed a regular stampede for seats. Fortunately we were aggressive enough to get ours, and after the scramble was over we found that, besides ourselves, there were a couple of enlisted men from the English Army in the compartment with us. At first they were cold and distant, but at last they smiled a little at some foolish thing that the three of us were laughing at.

"Wouldn't you like an American cigarette, soldier?" I asked, handing one of them the package. I remembered how Ivy, the little maid at our first barracks, had enjoyed them and how long it had been that she hadn't had any, and I thought they would enjoy one, too.

"Thank you, ma'am, we certainly would," he said, speaking for his friend. "They're mighty nice, and we haven't had one for quite some time."

As we talked with them, they were surprised to learn that we made more in one month than they earned in half a year. We found out that their home was in London, that they were returning on leave.

One of them was quiet for a moment and then said, "There isn't anything for me to go home for, really. My family were all killed in the blitz — all but my younger sister. She's crippled as a result of being injured, and her mind hasn't been normal since. I don't know as she will even recognize me when I see her."

Marjie reached into her bag and drew out a large bar of chocolate. "Do you think your sister would like this?" she asked. "It would be something for her to munch on, anyway."

The soldier's face brightened. "Chocolate! Shell love it. She's only eleven, you know, and we haven't had chocolate over here in months."

"If you ladies," said the friend, "will look over this way, you'll see we're coming to the outskirts of London."

We crowded over to the window to look, and it gave me a very sick feeling when we began to pass through sections that had been almost completely demolished by the bombs. Whole streets just swept clean. All the debris had been removed; but here and there would be just a single wall standing where formerly there had been a house. I couldn't help thinking that if some of the folks at home could ride through such an area of devastation, they would not be so complacent about the war.

At the station we bade our many soldier friends goodbye and started out to see London. We decided to take a cab to the American Nurses' Club, and the girl who evidently was trainmaster halted one for us. I had always thought I spoke the English language, but we had as much difficulty making the driver understand what we wanted as we were to have with the French later on. Our English was definitely not theirs. Finally we made him see what we wanted, and he started out while we craned our necks just like children afraid of missing something.

There were beautiful parks, now torn up with trenches for air-raid shelters. Every few feet along the road there were signs pointing the way to the various shelters, all of which were clearly marked as to how many people could be accommodated. I couldn't help contrasting these areas with Central Park in New York and the Boston Common — two famous sanctuaries in my own country for people who wanted leisurely to sprawl and rest in the sun. Not so here. Every available space was utilized as a means of protection from air attack. Practically everyone was riding bicycles, and there were no cars except the taxicabs. Gas — or petrol, as they call it — was very difficult to obtain, and the civilian population just didn't have cars any more.

Soon we turned into what must once have been a residential section, and there, straight ahead of us, extending out into the street over the entrance to a beautiful old stone front building, was Old Glory. Beside her was flying the flag of the American Red Cross. I swear I never looked at the American flag while away from the States that a lump didn't come up into my throat as I realized what it meant to be an American.

"Here you are, ladies," said the cab driver. "I hopes you'll enjoy your stay with us." He smiled a bit sadly for a second and then added, "Come back, ladies, after the war if you really wants to see what a jolly old country this is!"

We had quite a struggle paying him in shillings and sixpence, but it was finally settled to his satisfaction and to ours. We took our bags and went into the building. As we entered, a very pleasant Red Cross worker came out of what appeared to be an office and took our bags.

"Come on in, girls, make yourselves comfortable," she said in a good American accent. "We want you to make this your home while you're in London. How about a coke, now? And some jelly roll?"

"We'd love it," I said. "We haven't seen a coke since we left the States."

"I just can't believe this is true," sighed Millie. "I'm afraid if I pinch myself I'll find it's all a dream!"

"If you young ladies are quite refreshed," said our hostess after we had made away with great quantities of coke and jelly roll, "I'll show you to your room. It will cost five shillings, and that will include your bed, lunch, and breakfast in the morning. Is that satisfactory?"

"Why, that's just a little over a dollar!" I exclaimed. "Are you sure that's enough?"

She laughed and answered, "It really is. And we only want to pay our actual expenses of laundry and food — otherwise we'd not ask you a thing."

With this she took us to a room on the third floor. There were four small beds, but it so happened we didn't have a roommate. After hastily making our toilet, we met some officer friends from our reservation at the American officers' club for dinner.

On the way back, walking along in blackout, I asked, "Where's Piccadilly Circus?"

"I don't know for sure, but we'll ask the next bobby," Millie answered.

And we did, only to be told that Piccadilly Circus was precisely where we were at the time. The bobby (policeman to you!) made it furthermore very clear that almost anyone should have known that!

Thoroughly squelched, we walked along back to the Red Cross, tired but thrilled with the newly discovered life all around us.

London! We saw the changing of the guard at Buckingham Palace, the troops drilling at Wellington Barracks; Hyde Park, Westminster Abbey, St. Paul's Cathedral, Dickens' Old Curiosity Shoppe, Petticoat Lane, and everything else one sees in an orthodox Cook's tour. We had dinner at the Savoy and lunch at the Mayfair. Such linen, such silverware, and such service! But unfortunately very little food. Poor England, I discovered, was still living up to tradition, with so little to do it with. Late in the afternoon we took a cab to London's East End — the scene of the blitz. Whole city blocks flattened out into fields of rubble. When one thinks of what has happened to their homes, their businesses, their churches, and to their very families, you cannot help admiring and respecting the English people for their undaunted spirit after all the years and months of unbelievable hardship.

Soon it was time to leave for the train and camp, if we didn't want to be A.W.O.L. As we drove down through the city to the station, I knew I should never forget the sound of Big Ben as I heard him from Waterloo Bridge at midnight!

When we arrived at camp, everybody was milling around and talking together excitedly.

"What's new?" we all cried at once.

"The Colonel and Captain Proffitt, Major Snyder, and Major Mellies all received their promotions today," answered Vaughn Fisher.

"And the Chaplain, too," added Ginny Ayers. "Don't forget the Chaplain."

"We are going to have a party in the mess hall," said Kirk. "The orchestra from the field artillery outfit over on the hill is going to play for us. Say, that ought to be fun!"

And it was. We spent the evening dancing on a concrete floor and liking it! The Colonel had managed to snitch a little beer from somewhere, and I'll bet that was as good a promotion party as ever a group of men had. I even asked the Colonel to dance with me, which he did; and if I do say so myself, I don't think he minded in the least. We all went to bed a happy group of people in a strange but friendly land.

"Heavenly days!" exclaimed Louise in the morning. "Have you seen the bulletin board?"

"No, what is it? Something new and exciting?"

"I'll say so," answered Louise. "We aren't going to be allowed to take our foot lockers any farther. We are to pack our bedding rolls with the things we absolutely need, and the lockers are to go into storage here. Now isn't that indeed something?"

"Bedding rolls! Good Lord I can hardly close mine as it is, to say nothing of adding to it!" wailed Ann.

"And that isn't all," gloated Louise. "We are going on a dry run to practice loading for another train trip. No one will be excused. The entire outfit, nurses, doctors, and enlisted men are to go, wearing full field equipment, and the Colonel will set the cadence!"

"Now I've seen everything," cried Helen English, "send my body home and tell my mother that I loved her, will you?"

The next afternoon came all too soon, and the whole outfit lined up in front of headquarters and got ready to take off across country. We fell in, in formation, and I'll be darned if the Colonel didn't start checking to see if everyone had water in her canteen.

"Oh, my gosh! I didn't fill mine," exclaimed Edna Atkins. "Whatever am I going to do?"

"Just pray hell get tired before he gets to you!" replied Helen Molony.

At that Mary Meyer began to giggle.

"Quiet in the ranks!" roared the Colonel, none too sweetly. "Lieutenant Atkins, why isn't your canteen filled? You were given instructions, were you not?"

"Yes, sir," said poor Edna. "I guess I just forgot, sir."

"Forgot! That's a fine excuse, I must say. Don't ever let me hear any of you give it to me again. In the Army you don't forget. Understand?"

We all agreed that we did.

Then he called us to attention and started out. Over hill, down dale, on the road, off the road, and over fences — all in cadence. I swear I was just about deciding I could never make it when he called a ten-minute break. During the break he told us we would all be issued canned rations and chocolate bars when we returned to camp. He also told us our luggage must be ready to be picked up not later than four o'clock the following afternoon, and that we must be in formation, ready to go, at seven that night. That meant that the two-and-a-half-mile jaunt to the railroad station in the tiny town to our north must be made in blackout. I practically broke my confounded neck!

The next day arrived, and such a hustle and bustle as there was in camp, with everybody trying to take care of the last-minute details of packing! I don't think we had ever had better chow than we had for that last evening meal. I suspected they were trying to fatten us up for whatever the night might bring.

"Come on, girls, it's six-forty-five, and we have to be in formation in front of headquarters at seven," said Lieutenant Salter, Chief Nurse.

We stood there in the chill cold of early evening while final instructions were given our enlisted men. I remember the stars had never seemed so bright, nor so close, nor so personal! I am not particularly religious, but somehow as I stood there I seemed very close to my Maker, and I breathed a little prayer: Dear God, take care of us all. Let this mission be a success. Take care of Carlie and my mother and dad, and if anything happens to me, look after my boy. I do so much want him to grow up to be a fine young man in a world ruled by right and not might.

As we walked along through the darkness, not a sound could be heard. Soon we reached the limits of the town and then the railroad station. After a few minutes' wait for the train we climbed aboard with a minimum of confusion. I found that my seatmates were Whitey, Miss Hornback, and Miss Martin. Each of us received a paper sack containing sufficient rations to last us until we should reach our destination, wherever that might be. By the time we were loaded, everyone was trying to get as comfortable as possible, for we had learned on the first trip just how miserably tired we could get after a few hours of such travel. As the night passed, I kept waking Whitey up so that we might change our positions. Oh, my back and bones! I certainly felt every one of my thirty-three years at that point.

Then, when I felt I couldn't stand it any longer, we arrived.

CHAPTER FIVE: Life on an English Transport

Off the train at last, after an eighteen-hour, joint-stiffening trip. When I didn't have my knees in Whitey's ribs, she had hers in mine. If you've never tried to ride this length of time on an English train, with its tiny seats and cubbyhole compartments, let me tell you there's really nothing like it.

We stood there on Scottish soil in the cold of a late afternoon, a completely dejected lot of females. We were dirty, tired, and most of all — hungry. We had been given an apple and two sandwiches — Spam at that — when we left the camp site the day before.

After an hour and a half of waiting around doing nothing, our Colonel came hurrying along.

"Everybody on their toes, we're about to go aboard the lighter. There will be no unnecessary talking. And above all, no smoking. Step it up, now, we've no time to waste!"

The good old army game: hurry, hurry and wait! Finally, the line up ahead began to move. I fell over somebody's musette bag, and we started down the gangplank. Yes, down — because, believe it or not, that lighter was so tiny it stood below the level of the dock.

Little Edna Atkins, who measured five feet in her stockings and didn't weigh a bare hundred pounds, peered up at me from under her helmet. "Haskell, I'll never be able to make it. Once I get started down with this load on, gravity will just naturally take me to the bottom of the ocean."

I had to laugh, but I didn't blame her much for feeling that way. I was having a hard time holding myself back when I heard an excited voice yell, "Haskell, bon voyage, and behave yourself!" I looked up to see Captain Ray of the field artillery leaning over the side of another lighter just to the right of us.

It gave us a feeling of security to realize that many of our old friends from the military reservation in England were evidently bound for the same destination. Gradually, cautiously, and one by one, we made the trip down the gangplank and onto the greasy deck of the lighter. After we were herded into the bow of the thing, the enlisted men began to file on. They were from an engineering outfit and had survived an even longer train ride than we had.

Everyone was tired and tense, longing for that prohibited cigarette, when our CO. appeared on the scene, big as life and twice as natural.

The old adage about forbidden fruit certainly holds doubly true in the case of a cigarette. I don't believe I have ever wanted one more and the only consolation was the fact that we were all in the same fix.

Fortunately, we did not have long to brood about this minor discomfort, for our trip on the lighter was a short one and in a little while a banging and bumping told us we must have reached the transport. It was the signal to stand up and begin helping each other strap on packs and masks once again. We picked up our suitcases and started up a gangplank, in complete blackout. I banged the girl's legs ahead of me with my suitcase at the same time that the girl behind staggered into me with hers. I still wonder how we all made the deck without a casualty.

We were told to keep walking straight up until we reached A deck. We did, past rows and rows of grinning officers and members of the crew. For the first time in my life I was in a position where being a woman didn't seem to mean a thing. Here we were in the presence of men who had been made gentlemen and officers by act of Congress, and they were letting us struggle along under the weight of all we had on our backs — and carrying a suitcase besides. As if this wasn't enough in itself, they had to chip in such coy remarks as "Wow, what an army!" and "Now I've seen everything!"

I retorted, "So have I. You fellows are so busy learning to be heroes that you've forgotten how to be gentlemen!"

Needless to say, that produced offers to help us with our luggage — but we had already reached A deck on our own power. In the lounge, we flopped down eagerly into chairs; and as far as I was concerned at that moment, they could give it all back to the Indians.

Enter now a jaunty English female officer who came over and said, "Leave your luggage here, girls. You are to go below to the mess to eat."

Food, after being so many hours without it! We washed up hastily, then traipsed down three decks to the mess. Hot roast beef, fried potatoes, the inevitable cabbage, hard rolls, coffee, and steamed pudding. I sincerely hope those little English boys who served us didn't form their impressions of Americans from the way we wolfed our food that first night!

As our stomachs became filled, we began to wonder about the living accommodations. Upstairs our chief nurse awaited us with a list of the staterooms we were to occupy.

"Fill them up," she said stiffly. "Four girls to a room."

So we set about collecting our friends. I was walking along the companionway when Helen Molony, a freckle-faced Irish girl from upstate New York, stuck her head out of a door and said, "Hey, Rufus, come on in here with us." She had hardly spoken before she had my bag in hand and I was in.

The other two girls were little Atkins, whose home was in Green Bay, Wisconsin, and Mary Meyer, from Wapakoneta, Ohio. I'm sure you couldn't have found four girls of more widely divergent type if you had tried. But strangely enough, we got along well together. Helen was tall, about five feet ten, red-haired, freckled, slow and easygoing. Edna was tiny, fair complected, energetic and always on the move. Mary was our glamour girl. One of those sweet little wide-eyed females who has merely to lift her lovely long lashes to get a man. As for myself, I was just old Haskell, solid and good-natured, thirty-three years old, divorced and the mother of a beautiful ten-year-old son.

Inevitably there came the matter of deciding about bunks. Helen took one casual look and said, "Well, I certainly could not fold up my length in that upper, so I guess I better sleep on the lower level." This seemed a good piece of logic, and she proceeded to dump her luggage on the bunk.

Little Edna said, "I can probably climb up top easier than anyone else, so I'll take the top bunk on this side." Whereupon we promptly boosted her up to see how she would like it.

Mary and I looked at each other and grinned and decided we would take what was left.

That would have been well and good but for one factor we hadn't reckoned with. The transport, like all transports, had undergone certain changes in being converted into a troop ship. And after one got into one's bunk it became evident at once that there was no room to sit up! The process of rolling in and out of a bunk was really something to see. Edna did all right — she just climbed up like a monkey. And all Helen had to do was to sit down and roll in. But Mary and I — that was another matter. It took us three days at sea before we learned gracefully to crawl in and out on our tummies, then carefully turn over, and above all remember not to try to sit up.

Our second night out we had just quieted down to do some sleeping when I heard a terrific thump and then a subdued voice saying: "Judas

Priest!" I snickered and flashed on my light to see which one of us was the casualty.

Our Mary was standing out in the floor rubbing her forehead and giving the bunk a dirty look.

I said: "I guess maybe that isn't soft pine."

She replied "You're pretty good at guessing. But, say — what's a gal to do when she gets a nightmare? Wake up first and look around?"

She crawled back into her bunk and tried to settle down. But I realized she was restless and had something on her mind.

"Ruth," she whispered presently, "are you asleep?"

"No," I said. "What is it?"

"Are you — frightened?"

"Of course I am. Aren't you?"

You could almost hear the sigh of relief. She snuggled down for a minute and then said, "I wonder where we're going."

To this I had no intelligent answer.

"You know," she added sweetly, "I wouldn't mind this trip so much if I were sure I could use a return ticket."

This was the thing we were all thinking but were hesitant to put into words. Out of the mouths of babes come words of wisdom! I thought for a moment, then said, "Mary, the best thing you and I can do is to pray like the devil and hope for the best. Let's get some sleep."

I lay there wide awake like a hypocrite long after she and the others were snug in the arms of Morpheus. I thought of my young son at home with his grandparents in northern Maine. I missed him terribly. But I thought: Sonny, it's going to be worth the effort if it makes the world a better and safer place for you, and thousands of little boys and girls like you, to grow up in. With that comforting thought I, too, went to sleep wondering what the morrow might bring.

In the morning I went down to breakfast without my Mae West — life preserver to you! — and was promptly told off by the Chief Nurse. It developed that we were to have our first lifeboat drill that morning. So, before leaving the mess hall, we were assigned to our lifeboat stations.

As we had already had this type of drill coming over from the States to England, we weren't so hopelessly dumb as we were the first time. Luckily our station was just off the foyer on the deck where we slept.

"As you all well realize," boomed the nurse in a rich contralto, "we are in more danger than we have been since we left home. You must pay strict attention to what I have to say. When the bugler blows assembly, you are to go immediately to your lifeboat station wearing your overcoats, wool gloves, helmet, canteen belt, and canteen of water — and of course," she added, squinting at me, "your life preserver. I want each girl to have two ration bars in her overcoat pocket and her jackknife where she can get at it. Also it is well to have matches in some sort of waterproofed container. Do not have the chin strap of your helmet fastened as it might break your neck if you hit the water the wrong way. Also, do not forget to hold your life preserver firmly by the front straps until after you have immersed and come up again, for the same thing holds true here. If you make it a habit to go through the drill properly, you will be prepared to face the real thing — which can always be possible in these waters."

With these cheering words she went on her way, leaving us all rather quiet for a moment. Then, one by one, we rose and wandered out on deck to take a look at an ocean that could gleam and glisten so beautifully yet play host to such terrible tragedy. On either side of us the convoy moved lazily through water that was calm and serene. Hundreds of ships, thousands of human beings, all with one destination — and that unknown to most of us. It seemed hard to believe that within the very hour we might be at the mercy of the ocean — out there in a lifeboat or raft. I think every girl began to realize that we were now personally involved in the very real game of war.

At 10:30 A.M. the bugler blew assembly. (He must have been a fugitive from a dance band, for he made it sound more like the opening bars of Tiger Rag!) We all filed out and took our places at the rail. We were sixty nurses strong, and the stations were so arranged that there were five nurses, a doctor, and about thirty-five enlisted men to each lifeboat.

The enlisted men assigned to our boat were all husky members of a platoon of military police. I had never had much to do with M.P.'s, but I knew that these lads would be good to have around in a lifeboat — if one must be in a lifeboat!

There were thousands of personnel on that ship, but in exactly fourteen minutes the lifeboats could have been lowered over the side, if it had been necessary. Quite a comfortable feeling, I can tell you — knowing it could be done so fast!

That evening the "passenger list" gathered in the lounge off the boat deck to read, play cards, and write letters. Some of the girls tried knitting, others gathered around the piano for singing. I wasn't particularly interested in reading, didn't have any knitting, and singing has never been my forte. So I amused myself watching four boys play cribbage. That was one game I knew something about, and it became evident at once that one of the boys was a novice and the others were bent on taking him for a ride. Finally he gave up in disgust, slung down his cards on the table and left. This was the signal for the others to start laughing. One of them, who had noticed me kibitzing, turned around and said proudly, "How was that for a shellacking? We did all right I guess, eh?"

"Yes," I agreed icily, "if you call it good sportsmanship to gang up on some one who doesn't know the game."

The three of them looked at me in astonishment. The one who had spoken now colored and tugged at the corner of his collar. Doubtless eager now to gain the upper hand in a rather uncomfortable situation, he said, "Well, maybe you think you know this game."

I grinned sweetly. "Oh, I wouldn't say that. But I'll play a bit if you need a fill-in for your foursome."

They looked at each other, I thought rather wisely, and one of them reluctantly pulled out a chair for me. Fortunately the best player turned out to be my partner, and much to the chagrin of the other two — one of whom was my boastful friend — we trimmed them badly.

At this point the boy who had been my partner started grinning broadly. He studied me a moment, then said, "Say, how good a sport are you? Your commanding officer has asked me to play two-handed cribbage with him tonight. How'd you like to play in my place? And play to win."

Now, that was really putting me on the spot, for the Colonel was well known to me for the pride he took in winning at cards. But that grin was too much to resist, and I agreed.

The Colonel arrived in due time, and the young lieutenant told him I wanted to play.

"O.K. by me," he said, laughing good-naturedly, "if she wants to get a good beating!"

The saints were watching over me, for I beat him two games straight, then he beat me the third. He took a great deal of pleasure, all the rest of the trip, telling everybody how I beat him twice and then let him beat me because he was my boss!

That night passed uneventfully. Though somehow the ocean appeared to be getting restless — or could it have been my tummy?

The first thing I heard after falling asleep was the pleasant voice of Pennington, our English steward, "Wake up young ladies, it's seven o'clock." Yes, it was really morning!

Pennington was a man in his early sixties, with a fringe of white hair around a very pink bald head. He was kindly, friendly, genial — all the things rolled into one that I have ever read or heard about English servants. Somewhere along the way he had acquired a grand sense of humor and could enjoy a joke as well as the next one, even though it might be on himself.

Four very sleepy voices answered "O.K.," and he went on his way, only to return in a very few minutes and say: "Come now, ladies, you'll miss breakfast."

Instantly I knew that that was the answer to the whole thing. The way that ship was tossing around, I didn't care if I never ate again as long as I lived.

"Go away," I wailed. "I'm sick, and I don't ever want any breakfast again."

On the other side of the room Mary said in a very weak voice, "I know I can never make it to get to mess."

Edna went skinning down by me like a monkey and proceeded to make her toilet while I watched her out of one eye and wondered how anyone could be so disgustingly cheerful.

In a couple of minutes Helen rolled her long length out of her bunk, blinked a second, and said, "Morning? I swear that I just went to bed. By the way, Haskell, did you beat the Colonel?" (Talking about a card game when I was becoming more sure by the minute that I was approaching death's door!) Then her expression changed and she became very indignant. "Do you know what I heard up in the lounge last evening?" Before we could answer she went on, "One of those English officers said he didn't see any earthly use for women on the ship, considering its destination. Said he didn't see how they could possibly be anything but a hindrance, and for that matter women on board ship were an ill omen anyhow, and he didn't believe we'd ever reach our objective without trouble."

"Better hurry. You'll be late for breakfast," I said, but nothing could stop her once she was started.

"Not only that," she continued excitedly, "but our own officers didn't stand up for us. Now, how do you like it?"

I, for one, was too sick to care, but Edna just glared and muttered under her breath something about "We'll show them!"

About that time Pennington came back with the hot water. Fresh water on board ship is rationed, and we only got it once a day. As he reached through the door to place the jug on the floor, he discovered me still in my bunk.

"What seems to be the matter?" he asked. "You know, if you aren't in the dining room on time you won't get any breakfast."

There he was again, talking about food when it certainly was the last thing I wanted to hear mentioned. "Oh, Pennington," I confessed, "I couldn't eat if my life depended upon it. I'm seasick."

"On this mill pond?" he answered, incredulous.

I swear I could have killed him if I could have found the strength.

He laughed as though it was a very monstrous joke and said, "Look here now, miss, you mustn't give in to it. Get up and dress and go down to eat, and then get out into the fresh air."

The girls now joined into the plan, eagerly, and there was nothing for me to do but drag myself out and struggle into my slacks and sweater. Believe me, it was a struggle.

I went to the mess. But when the ship gave a sudden lurch to port side and then shuddered down off the crest of a wave, I left in a hurry. Back I rushed to my stateroom, my one living desire being to get horizontal again.

I hadn't much more than made it when back came Pennington. Personally, I don't know what I would have done without him during those next few days. He brought me hard rolls to chew on and apples to munch. But I felt like an awful sissy. Here was I, the biggest, huskiest one of the lot — flat on my back. But seasickness, like love, isn't at all particular where it strikes.

Finally I managed to struggle out for a little air — but not for long. The deck was squirming like a snake. Back I staggered to the stateroom, convinced that a little more bed rest was needed. There was still a pretty heavy sea running, and as I made the effort to get into my bunk — which was about six feet off the floor — the ship lurched again. When it did, I had my foot on the lower bunk and my other knee on the one above. I was thrown off balance and landed on the floor, flat on my back, with a dull, sickening thud.

In rushed Pennington, bless him. He helped me into the bunk. I saw stars of every shape and color, and oh, what a headache! As a result Edna and

Helen had to lift me in and out of my bunk for several days, but I guess that scared the seasickness out of me, for I was beginning to believe I would live.

At last came the day when we found out where we were going. Northwest Africa, of all places! We were issued mosquito cream, head nets, netting for our cots, tablets to chlorinate water with, atabrine tablets for malaria, salt tablets, and tiny American flags to be sewn upon the sleeves of our jackets when we went ashore. We also received little booklets telling us about the customs of the people, what to do and also — what was more important — what not to do after we landed.

The Colonel cautioned us against losing any of this issue, and we all retired to the lounge. There quite a discussion was going on. One high-ranking American officer was saying, "I knew we shouldn't have these girls aboard. They'll be more trouble than they're worth." Another: "I'm glad my sister isn't here. She wanted to join the Army, and I wouldn't let her!" From all sides, comments were flying. And the girls themselves, who should have been the ones concerned about their welfare, weren't saying a word! The more these men talked, the more indignant we became.

Finally Louise Miller, a meek little girl from Selma, Alabama, spoke up and addressed the officer nearest our group. "Why don't they give us a chance to see what we can do before they start condemning us? We volunteered for this job, and we'll see it through. Yes, and without the help of all the officers who are fussing about it. When the going gets tough, I guess you'll find that we will carry our own weight!"

There was an electric silence, and then an English officer spoke up. "I believe the young lady has something there. Maybe we better wait and see how this all turns out before we begin to criticize."

That same morning at boat drill the CO. of Troops explained the procedure of going ashore once we reached our destination. He said:

"Men, most of you have practiced landing operations from Higgins craft at one time or other, but that is not true of the medical group aboard. For their benefit I will explain the procedure. You will go ashore in exactly the same formation you are in now. Five nurses, one medical officer, and twenty enlisted men. On the signal you will proceed down over the side of the ship on the iron ladder and step off onto the landing barge. Here is where you must be careful. Do not step off as the barge is falling down in the trough of the wave; wait until it rises. Push well up into the front of the barge to make room for those coming behind you, and then turn and face the man in charge. These craft cannot get in close to shore and will go in as close as possible, when the back will be let down. Everyone step off into the water, go ashore, be absolutely quiet, and get under whatever cover there is to be had as soon as possible."

I imagine that the expressions on the faces of the girls were something to behold, as I caught one big burly M.P. with a very knowing grin on his face. I suppose they thought: Well, here is where those girls will break, now that they realize what they're in for.

God love every girl in the nurses' group. No matter what they might have been thinking, they kept their chins up, eyes front, and didn't bat a lash. Somehow you could perceive a growing respect in the eyes of the male officers who had been fussing about our not being able to take it.

We were wending our way slowly back to the foyer when Anne Cooney, a little Irish girl from Boston, Massachusetts, spoke up. "Heck, I never did like to wear a bathing suit in swimming."

Everybody roared, and from then on in the quips flew thick and fast, but never a complaint. We were all frightened. It was only natural. But each girl was keeping that fear to herself. Of course, what the CO. failed to mention was that we were to do all this under fire. That, evidently, was supposed to be a mere incidental. . . .

We were getting into very dangerous waters by this time, and everyone was tense and apprehensive. All hands were out on deck, and we had just been watching some of the enlisted men doing calisthenics when there was a queer shudder that seemed to pass through the very body of the ship. One of the ship's officers informed us that a vessel in the convoy must have fired a depth charge at a submarine, and the shudder was the result of the explosion. That didn't serve to make us feel any better, I can assure you. We had seen corvettes firing off their ash cans at the edge of the convoy before, but never near enough for us to feel the explosion.

That evening there was much forced gaiety in the lounge. Commander George Burnham of the Navy, whose home was in Baltimore, Maryland, came along to our group and told us that we should be sighting the lights of Tangier soon. Inasmuch as Tangier was a neutral country, it wouldn't be blacked out. He and I left for the boat deck and stood by the rail watching the starlight, when we were joined by several of the nurses and doctors. Sure enough, right ahead of us, Tangier's lights began to glow. It seemed so strange that after all those weeks of complete blackout we should see lights so plainly.

Commander Burnham, who had sailed those waters many times, was pointing out to me the shadow that was the celebrated Rock of Gibraltar when suddenly, from overhead, came the ominous drone of a plane.

I said, "Commander, what's that? One of ours — I hope."

He listened for a minute, then said calmly, "I don't believe it is a Jerry. It doesn't quite sound like one."

At just that minute the plane dropped a flare, and the entire convoy was silhouetted for about a minute and a half. We immediately dropped down below deck level, as our faces would be plainly discernible in the bright light. Breathless moments passed before the flare extinguished itself and darkness once more prevailed.

We straightened up again, and for a while no one said a word. Then one of the medical officers said, "What do you think, Commander?"

Another chimed in, "Is that going to make trouble for us?"

One of the girls spoke up and said, "I'm scared."

"You and me both!" I said, taking her arm.

It could have been just a friendly plane, or it might have been a reconnaissance plane for the enemy. Whatever it was, it didn't leave us feeling any too happy, because we were definitely in "hot" territory at this time.

Finally we all went back in and joined the group at the piano at their singing. But there certainly wasn't a song in our hearts. From down in the foyer below someone had resurrected a victrola and some records, and the younger officers and nurses were dancing. We joined them; and as I sat down to rest between records, I happened to sit beside an English major.

He said, "I wouldn't have believed it!"

"Believed what?" I asked.

He looked at the girls laughing up at the boys, dancing with them, and replied, "Look—dancing, laughing, and having fun as though they didn't have a care in the world, when they are only about thirty-six hours away from the most momentous event of their lives." He looked at me curiously and asked, "Aren't you afraid?"

"Of course," I confessed. "But it's too late to do anything about it now. I'll go ahead and try to do a good job, and pray like blazes that we make it."

He watched the dancers a few moments in silence. Then he turned to me and held out his hand. "May God bless you, young lady. You Americans certainly have what it takes to make you the splendid nation that you are!"

At this point the voice of the captain of the ship came over the loud-speaking system: "Fellow Americans, we are nearly at our destination. May God watch over you and make this mission a success. We have enjoyed bringing you down here and, God willing, we will be glad to take you back when this is all over — when right instead of might rules the nations once again!"

I cleared a lump in my throat and noticed that the eyes around me were suspiciously bright as he stopped speaking. Just for a minute, and then — on with the dance.

In my diary that night I scribbled hurriedly: "November 7, our last day out. An air of determination prevails about the ship, and everyone is at that last-minute job of wishing friends good luck, packing the last end of personal belongings, and getting final instructions about what to do when we finally get around to disembarking. To bed, but I am afraid not to sleep. Anything may happen from here on in. We have orders to rise for a four-thirty breakfast. Heavenly days, what an hour! Wonder what tomorrow will bring — not only to myself but to my nation?"

CHAPTER SIX: We Reach Our Destination at Last

It was 4:30 a.m. I stirred restlessly and then awakened quickly at the sound of artillery fire in the distance. This was the day we were to go into Africa. It seemed the French were to give us some opposition although it hadn't been expected they would.

"Edna," I asked. "Are you awake?"

"Yes," came a breathless reply. "Did you hear that? I wonder what's going on outside? I'd hate to miss anything at this stage of the game."

"We'll go have a look," I said, waking Mary and Helen who were sleeping like babes in the wood.

We had begun to dress hurriedly, talking all the while, when the Chief Nurse stuck her head in through the door.

"You are to report to the mess hall at once for breakfast. As soon as you have finished, you are to return to your rooms or to the lounge. The troops are going ashore, and they do not want us in the way."

At mess that morning we had neither the time nor the inclination to indulge in pleasantries. The men were in battle dress. Leggings, cartridge belts, canteens of water, gas masks, steel helmets — the whole works. They wore rather grim expressions. This was the moment we had all been trained for. The din offshore was becoming louder as we reached our destination, and we were so consumed with curiosity that it was hard to obey orders about staying inside.

"How is your courage, young lady?" asked an English major with whom I had become quite friendly. "Are you ready for what lies ahead?"

"Frankly," I confessed, "I'm scared to death. But there doesn't seem to be anything that I can do about it now."

"Better eat a good breakfast, girls," ventured the waiter. "You don't know when you'll be eating your next meal."

At that moment a loud blast rattled the windows above us in the mess hall.

"Wow, that one was close," piped up our commanding officer, who had arrived to give us final orders.

We were to be ready to go ashore at any time after eleven. We were to have on all our warm clothing and to check our canteens to be sure they were filled with water.

"The gunfire," explained the officer, "is apparently coming from Oran. We are to land about twenty miles this side. A little harbor town called Arzeu. It will be impossible to get into the harbor, so the entire personnel of this ship is to go aboard the Higgins landing craft, from which it will be necessary for you to wade ashore. You have already been instructed to get under whatever cover there may be and to be silent. I know I can depend upon you to obey orders. Don't fail me, because in doing so you will be failing yourselves." He smiled at us all as he added, "Seriously, girls, you are behaving better than most of the men. They seem to be troubled with jitters already. I'm proud of you. Take care of yourselves, and may God bless you!"

There was a constant rumble now of heavy gunfire offshore, and we could hear the voices of the enlisted men as they were going down over the sides into the waiting barges. We returned to our staterooms, where we made the exciting discovery that by opening the portholes we could partially view the proceedings. Such young faces, and all lined alike with fear and anxiety. Only the voices of the platoon sergeants could be heard, now, giving orders. Self-preservation being one of the first instincts we know, I need not blush to admit I was frightened. And I know very well that the rest of the girls were, too.

"Have you a cigarette, Haskell? Mine are all gone," said Edna.

"I have some somewhere," I replied and started looking in my musette bag for the spare packages I had stored there.

"Have one of mine," said Helen, handing me her pack. "Seems to me we're doing a lot of chain smoking this morning!"

I laughed a little. "This is one time all cigarettes taste alike. Just so they're stuffed with tobacco."

We began making last-minute preparations for leaving the stateroom. Then we heard the Chief Nurse saying to someone down the hall,

"Girls, the CO. says we may go out onto the starboard side of A deck if we want to. They are loading the troops from B deck just below us. He thinks we may not get so jittery if we have something to take up our minds."

We all reached the door at the same time, carrying our personal belongings with us and agreeing that the CO. had something there. In the hall the Chief Nurse regarded us with amazement, much as though she suspected us of using mental telepathy.

From the rail of A deck we looked down over the side. Two barges were in the process of being loaded. One was directly under the iron ladder that swings out from the side of the ship, and the second was being boarded from a rope ladder which swung freely over the side. I thought: Here's hoping we go down that iron job. I knew I'd surely break my neck trying to go down the rope with a pack on my back!

As we stood there kibitzing, one of the helmeted figures looked up, smiled, clasped his hands together in a gesture of farewell, and then waved at me. It was Major Browning, of one of the engineering groups; and true to real Army tradition, he was going in with his men.

Soon the barge swung away from the transport with its load and started toward shore. Nearly all the men looked up and waved as the distance between the transport and the barge widened.

"Why, you can't see the shore!" I exclaimed, as the barges faded from sight.

"They're running through a smoke screen — that's why," volunteered one of the soldiers from the deck below.

Sure enough, the entire harbor was covered with a smoke screen, which served as protection both for the troops going in and for the ships standing idle in the harbor. At one point the screen was thinning out, and a small craft circled around, then fired a white phosphorous bomb from a rifle set up on the deck. As it struck the water, smoke began pouring forth, and in just a split second a complete screen was formed once again.

Barge and barge was loaded; and as each group swung away from the transport, it would look up, as one man, and wave.

"You know, I think it's doing those boys good to have you girls to wave to," said the Chaplain, who was standing beside us. "Gives them a sense of having somebody who cares where they're going and whether they get through. I think you should have been allowed on deck before."

The sound of the gunfire grew louder and seemed to be coming nearer. We were glad when finally the Chief Nurse arrived and told us she wanted to speak to us in the foyer. In groups of two and three we returned inside, where the thunder of the guns seemed distant once again.

"We are to go over the side at about two-thirty this afternoon," she informed us. "I am now going to assign you to groups in the manner in which you are to board the craft. There will be five nurses, two medical officers, and twenty of our enlisted men. When I have finished reading off the names, find your boatmates and stick closely to them so that when the time comes to go ashore there will be no uncertainty. You were instructed by the CO. of Troops how to board these craft. Again, be sure that you wait for the craft to rise from the trough of the wave before you attempt to step off the iron ladder." At mention of the word "iron" you could hear a very audible sigh of relief go up from those assembled.

"The first girl in each group," she continued, "will be in charge of the nurses in her barge. Lieutenant Haskell, Lieutenant Cooney, Lieutenant MacDonald, Lieutenant Ferree, and Lieutenant Williams are to go in the barge with Captain Kingston and Captain Sutton. When they call for Group Two, you five girls are to go to the head of the iron ladder and wait for the two medical officers and the enlisted men assigned to your group. Are there any questions?"

When she had finished assigning the girls by groups, we were eager to go out on deck again. At least the rope ladder no longer seemed such a menace, though the guns still roared. A group of coast artillery soldiers were going over the side, each man carrying a part of a machine gun on his shoulders, besides his regular equipment. I thought at the time that if anyone was unfortunate enough to fall overboard, he surely would go to Davy Jones's locker in a hurry just from the weight of such a load. Many of us girls had surgical instruments and bandages to look after, but nothing to compare with what these men were carrying.

I began to dread the thought of having to put a pack on my back, because it — the back — had been troubling me as a result of the fall from my bunk. While bracing my nerves for the inevitable moment, I noticed that, over to the port side of us, one of the destroyers suddenly circled in nearer shore. She broke through the smoke screen and, almost as soon as she had disappeared from view, fired a round from one of her three-inch guns. We all watched anxiously, and soon she stuck her nose through the screen of smoke once again and sailed by us nonchalantly. A brace of salvos from the gun of a French ship could be heard in the distance, and then quiet once again. That was enough, however, to prove they were ready and waiting for us. We exchanged pointed glances and then, almost as if obeying a command, reached for our cigarettes.

"All right, girls, are you ready?" shouted the Chief Nurse, excitedly. "They are going to take the medical unit ashore. I am going in the first craft with the Commanding Officer and the Adjutant. The girls who were assigned to go with me, go at once to the head of the ladder. As for the rest of you, chins up, and I'll see you on shore."

Group Two, of which I was part, congregated in one spot and began fastening packs and gas masks. As Cooney finished closing the clasp on mine, and as the weight of the thing settled upon my body, I involuntarily groaned. Luckily nobody heard me.

One by one we lined up at the rail, stealing apprehensive glances at the barge below.

"Are you ready. Lieutenant Haskell? Are your girls all here?" asked Captain Sutton, who was in charge.

"All here, ready and waiting, sir!" I answered.

"Good. Remember all you have been told about going aboard these barges. Keep your mind clear and alert, and above all do not stumble after you start down the ladder. I'm going on ahead and will help you in over the side of the barge. Chins up, youngsters, this is it!"

I looked hastily around for the girls I had shared the stateroom with and found that Edna had gone in the barge with Lieutenant Salter, the chief nurse, and that the others were scattered in different groups. We grinned and waved, and then started down the ladder.

"Lordy, I'll never be able to make it, Anne," said Jane Ferree as she stepped down behind me. "I'm scared to death. Being up so high makes me dizzy, and I can't swim a stroke!"

Anne Cooney chuckled and replied,

"Jane, honey, the way this ocean is moving up and down, I don't think any of us would be able to swim much if we had to."

"Are you all right, girls?" asked Captain Kingston, who was at the head of the ladder giving a helping hand.

"Yes, sir," replied Phyllis MacDonald. "But I'll feel a whole lot better when I'm finally in that barge. I just don't cotton to the idea of stepping off the bottom of this ladder. That space between the transport and the barge looks terribly wide from here."

"O.K., ma'am, give me your hand."

I looked up and into the face of an English sailor, one of the crew of the barge, who had his hands outstretched to assist me in.

I reached out for his hand, and as I did so the barge dipped down into the trough of the biggest wave I had ever seen. Lordy! The lad who had been standing directly beside me a few seconds before was now laughing up at me from a distance of seven or eight feet below. My heart pirouetted and my knees bumped together, but I knew there wasn't any sense in stalling, so when the barge rose again on the wave I grasped his hand, closed my eyes, and stepped off hopefully into space. I guess I didn't miscalculate, because the next second he had his hands under my armpits swinging me down into the belly of the thing.

"That wasn't so bad, now, was it, young loidy?" he asked.

Before I had a chance to answer, he was swinging Jane along beside me. She was a little white around the mouth but came up grinning.

"Imagine meeting you here," she laughed. "We certainly do get around, don't we?"

Just then there was a loud clap of gunfire from the direction of the shore, and we quickly stopped smiling. Soon the rest of the girls, and the enlisted men, were on, and we swung away from the transport. As I glanced up toward the rail, the soldiers who were still on board waved their hands in farewell, and many of them raised their hands briskly to their helmets in a salute as one soldier to another.

"Turn and face the other way," ordered Captain Sutton. "As soon as the sailor lets down the ramp at the back, I want everybody to step off into the water and go directly ashore. You men, stick by these girls until we learn what is to happen next."

"Have a smoke, Lieutenant?" asked a young corporal.

"Thanks, soldier," I stammered. "I guess I need one badly."

Captain Kingston now ordered us to crouch a little lower in the boat, as we were getting in closer to shore. It was possible to make out clearly several cottages which stood up on pilings — looking too peaceful to be true. Of course, from our point of observation, it was impossible to see the snipers who were hiding among them!

"O.K., everybody on their toes. Be ready to step off as soon as the ramp is dropped." This, at long last, from the English sailor at the helm.

There was the rasp of metal against metal, the back of the barge was dropped, and the enlisted men stepped off into the water.

I gasped as the first man almost entirely disappeared — the ocean coming up to his armpits. Then one of the taller boys stepped off and turned around.

"Let me have your hand, Lieutenant Haskell," he said. "Maybe I can help a little!"

I took one look at the swirling sea and reached for him, stepping off the barge at the same time. I shuddered as the ice cold water began seeping through my heavy clothing.

The soldier kept his arm around my waist until my feet touched bottom, and then I struggled the rest of the way unaided while he turned back to help one of the other girls. As I reached the sand, the weight of my pack became apparent and my poor old back began aching. I staggered over a stretch of beach and dropped down under the steps of a cottage about a hundred yards away. It was then that I heard for the first time the ping of a sniper's rifle which, on this occasion, kicked up a chunk of sand on the path along which I had trodden.

Edna and the rest of the girls joined me under the cottage as the barges continued to come ashore. We were crouched there together, having a smoke and keeping on the alert for snipers, when the CO. arrived, much disturbed because we had been put ashore a mile and a half from the point where we were scheduled to land. There was the occasional boom of heavy artillery far inland; but strangely enough, this didn't seem to register in our minds quite as much as it had when we first began to hear it in the early hours of the morning.

A rather tired-looking boy was walking guard on the beach directly in front of the cottage under which we were huddled. It seems he was a member of a ranger battalion that had come ashore before dawn and had met with plenty of trouble from Arab snipers. He told us that heavy fighting was taking place a little farther inland. "There are plenty of casualties," he said, "at the battalion aid station up town. And not a great deal of help to take care of them."

I suspected then that we had our night's work cut out for us.

"Fall in! Single file and well dispersed," barked Colonel Ringer when the men had disposed of the snipers along the beach front. "Be on the lookout for trouble, and drop down quickly if you are shot at. We have to go up to the point where we were supposed to have landed. We will walk along the sand so as to be out of range from the top of that hill."

As the Colonel finished speaking, he started out at the head of the line with Major Proffitt following close behind. We fell in, with the enlisted men dispersed among the nurses. I finally got my pack on my back and dropped into place behind the others.

When we reached the appointed spot, the barges were already unloading vehicles, and it surely looked funny to see one of the amphibious jeeps drive directly off into the water and proceed up the beach like any other dry land motorcar.

"Everybody under this building," ordered the Colonel, directing us to a weather-beaten cottage not much different from the one down the beach.

Again we crawled under on hands and knees and squatted down for a smoke on the sand. I, for one, was exhausted, and it was becoming dusky and cold. We huddled together for warmth and kept as quiet as possible, for we didn't want to cause any trouble that could be attributed to a woman's talking too much!

"I'm starving," said Millie Harris. "Haskell, I haven't talked to you in weeks. What do you think of this little picnic we are on?"

"I was never one for picnics," I said, "so I really wouldn't know."

"You girls might as well eat some of the rations you have in your packs," said the Chief Nurse, crawling in among us. "I think we are to stay here on the beach for the night. Captain Forman came in earlier this morning with the Corps Surgeon to try to find a place for us under cover, but as yet he hasn't succeeded."

I noticed she was holding on to a bar of concentrated chocolate. Soon everybody was eating rations of one type or another. Two girls got together on one can, in most instances, for a can of almost anything was enough for two portions.

Just then Mary Meyer crawled over to me, looking rather worried.

"Have you seen Molony?" she whispered, "She was in Lieutenant Schwade's barge, and he doesn't seem to be around. Do you know who the other girls were who were assigned to that group?"

I thought for a minute and said, "I think Doris Friedlund is one of them. Is she around?"

Lieutenant Salter decided to go looking for the Colonel, because it now became evident that some of us were missing.

Edna and Mary and I sat there talking together in low tones and wondering what might have happened to Molony and her group. We were more worried than we cared to admit to each other. Just about the time we were beginning to lose hope, along came the disheveled figure of Helen Molony looking very tired and wet.

"For heaven's sake, where have you been?" I asked.

"Yes, what happened?" asked Edna and Mary in unison.

"Oh, Lord, I don't know," answered Helen in rather a disgusted voice. "First we had engine trouble and drifted a few miles off the course. Then it began to get dusky, and we had no running lights, and finally they put us ashore in water nearly over our heads." She stopped a second and laughed heartily. "You should have seen Friedlund. She is so short that she practically drowned when she first stepped off, and then one of the boys helped her to shore and she liked it much better."

At this point Doris crawled under the cottage, resembling a drowned rat. She was pretty peeved about it, too, and didn't like it very much when we giggled at her appearance. I'm sure the rest of us didn't look much better, at that. Only we had reached the point where we no longer cared.

We gave them cigarettes and shared our rations with them. Doris' sunny nature soon revived, and Molony had already reached normal when the Chief Nurse told us we were to sleep in one of the deserted cottages on the beach.

We all crawled out now and walked the several yards down the beach to our new quarters. The guns rumbled in the distance, but we hardly noticed them now. As we filed up the steps in the semidarkness, a couple of enlisted men who had been removing debris from the floor came out, laughing as though they shared some monstrous joke. The building was divided into two rooms, and as the hospital unit was to work in two groups we were separated as such that night. It was rapidly becoming dark, and we weren't allowed to have lights, so we tried to place our equipment where we would know what we had done with it.

"Let's go outside, Haskell," suggested Glenna Whitt. "I'm not sleepy, and it's so dark and crowded in here. Besides, it's only six-thirty, and that's no hour to go to bed, is it?"

"I'll go with you two if you don't mind," added Louise Miller.

"May we go outside?" I asked the Chief.

"It's O.K. with me," she said. "Only don't wander away where you might get into serious trouble. Remember, there's to be absolutely no smoking. And don't use your flashlights in this building. They would make an excellent target for snipers. I hear there are still a great many of them about."

The three of us wandered out onto the steps and sat down to watch the activity around us. All the ships in the harbor were lighted at stern and bow, and the ones nearer the shore, which were in the process of being unloaded, had floodlights on to help them unload. One could hear the chug of the bulldozer working farther down the beach, pounding the sand down so that the vehicles that were being unloaded might run ashore without so much difficulty. The sky would be bright as day, at intervals, with the flare of the bursting shells. There was the occasional sound of a sniper's rifle and then the subdued oaths of the soldiers as they scattered and dropped to the ground.

An extraordinarily helpless feeling prevails in any medical group at such a time. We were technically noncombatants and unarmed. But we knew that someone out there in the darkness whom we could not see was taking pot shots at us, and we could not retaliate. All the personnel at our particular point were of our outfit and therefore not armed. As each combatant group came ashore, it immediately pushed on toward the thick of the fighting, and there we sat like God's stepchildren. Just then the two boys who had been doing the cleanup job in our home for the night came up and asked if there was anything they could do.

"I certainly hope you girls sleep well," volunteered one of them. And then, as his glance met his friend's, they both went off into a gale of laughter.

"What on earth is so funny?" I asked. "I noticed you fellows looked awfully wise as we went into the cottage this evening. Come on now, give."

They chuckled for a bit, then proceeded to tell us they had had to remove five dead and blood-bespattered Arabs from the floor before we could take over the cottage.

"If you sleep one-half as well as they were sleeping when we moved them out, I guess nothing will disturb you!" said one, by way of cracking wise.

Shades of my Irish ancestors! I had expected most anything but this. Sleeping in a temporary morgue for dead snipers was not my idea of comfort; but then I remembered that my dad had always said, it wasn't a dead man you should fear but a live one!

When we did get up enough nerve to retire for the night, it was evident we must sleep on the floor. Of course there was the table, but none of us cared to hog such luxury — and it was only large enough for one.

"I smell dead Arabs," said Louise, sniffing noisily as we laid ourselves out on what available space still remained on the floor.

"So long as they're dead," I said, proudly quoting my father as I curled up beside Edna, whose things were with mine.

Thus began our first night in a foreign country. I wondered what morning would bring.

CHAPTER SEVEN: Under Fire

Here we were, huddled down on the tile floor of a deserted beach house, while outside was the steady sound of artillery fire and the sky bright as day, at times, with the light from the bursting mortar shells. Our only piece of furniture was a rectangular table which stood in the center of the room. All the windows in the place had either been shot out or broken from concussion, and it was rapidly becoming cold, very cold. Our clothing was still damp from the ducking we had received in the Mediterranean, and we had no cover.

Edna and I were tucked in, as well as could be possible with our overcoats, on the floor directly under the table. Tired as we were, it was impossible to think of sleeping.

Over in the corner some girl said, "Simmons ought to be shot for making a mattress as hard as this one!" Another remarked, "I know I'm going to have the print of the floral design in this confounded floor on my backsides!" About that time Doris Friedlund, a demure little miss from Gary, Indiana, looked around her and said, "I guess if anyone wants to turn over during the night we'll have to do it 'by the numbers!'" (This was a howl, as Doris was the one girl in the group who never could master close-order drill.)

Gradually we became quiet, but we did not go to sleep. It grew colder as the floor grew harder — by the minute! Edna had just finished wiggling around trying to get comfortable, when the back door flew open and the Colonel's voice boomed out in the darkness.

"Atkins, Kelly, and Haskell. Report to headquarters immediately. Wear all your equipment, and bring your gas masks!"

Bang! the door went shut, and we could hear him hurrying away toward headquarters. There wasn't a sound for a second, and then Atkins rolled out from under the table on one side and I on the other.

We began to scramble around frantically in the dark trying to find our canteen belts, packs, and so forth. We learned one good lesson right there: Never let your equipment get away from you, because the Lord only knows under what kind of circumstances you'll be hunting for it later.

"I wonder where you are going?" someone said uneasily.

Then another voice: "Why aren't we all going? Why only you three?"

Louise Miller came over and helped me strap my pack on, and messed around until she found my helmet. In the meantime one of the other girls had been helping Edna and Kelly.

Kelly said, "Well, girls, guess this is it. We're on our way. Are you ready?"

"I've got rubber knees," Edna said, "but I guess I'm ready. How about you, Haskell?"

I stumbled over one of the girls in the darkness. "Here I am," I said. "Where do we go from here?"

There were cries of "Take care of yourselves," "Good luck, you brats," and "Save something for us to do when we get there."

We stepped over girls and equipment, and just as we got to the door someone threw an arm around my shoulder, I heard a sob, and then: "Take care of yourself, you damned Yankee!" The sky was bright for a second from a burst of a shell, and I looked back to see Louise standing there, her eyes bright with tears. My little Rebel friend from Alabama, who had teased me so much about being a Yankee! This made a lump come in my throat the size of a golf ball.

We groped our way down the steps, and one of the enlisted men was waiting there to take us to headquarters about a hundred yards away in another ancient cottage. Finally we made it, after stumbling through the sand and waking up a couple of the boys who were asleep on the ground trying to catch a few seconds of much-needed rest.

Once inside the building, which was lighted only by a kerosene lamp, we found the Chief Nurse, our Colonel, and the Corps Surgeon, who had come in from a small village four miles away. "All Hell's to pay up the line," said the Colonel, "and we have to have help. The boys at the battalion aid station can't handle the casualties, they're coming so fast."

Just as he finished talking, the door burst open again and in came two of our surgeons.

Captain Borgemyer said, "What's it all about, what's up!"

Captain Markham just beamed his genial smile and waited for someone to volunteer the information as to why he had been called out of his nice comfortable foxhole.

The Chief Nurse gave each of the three of us a box of morphine surrettes and a hypo syringe.

"Goodness knows what you will find up there," she said. "But do as good a job as you can, and at least these will help those God-blessed boys if the pain gets too bad."

The two surgeons had a supply of sedatives and narcotics, and at last we started off — an eerie little procession of three girls and four men. The jeep, we understood, had been left some distance back from where we were bivouacked.

It was very difficult to walk in the loose and sliding sand, especially as we seemed to be walking uphill. You couldn't see your hand before you, until all of a sudden the sky would be bright for just a second as another shell reached its mark. The backs of my legs were beginning to ache, and I began to understand why the Colonel had insisted on our drilling and having road marches back in England.

Just then there was a queer whistling sound, and the enlisted man on ahead said quickly, "Down!"

Before I had a chance to drop, he had pushed me by the shoulder and down I went.

"What was that?" I asked.

"Damned sniper somewhere taking a pot shot at us. The dirty bastard!"

Surely such doings were not to be taken lightly, and I'll confess that when I got back onto my feet and we started on again, I did so with a very queer feeling around my heartstrings.

Kelly and Atkins were both little girls, and I was a great big husky brute. I wondered how they were standing it, because I knew that I, for one, was getting plenty tired. In fact I had just about decided I would drop from exhaustion, when a dark object loomed up in front of us that turned out to be the jeep.

Now, I had driven one of the things in the States and been joy-riding in them in England. But I certainly felt more apprehension about swinging my slack-covered leg up over the side of this one than any other one I had ever laid eyes on.

I got in first, and then Captain Borgemyer tossed first Edna in behind me and then Kelly. The rest of the party got in, and we started off, a soldier with a tommy gun on each front fender. Somehow I didn't know whether to feel better or worse about their being there. I must confess my emotions were rather mixed at this point. Then I discovered that the man riding behind us also held a tommy gun protectingly in the corner of his arm. Shades of my Irish ancestors!

We drove maddeningly along for a few hundred yards, when suddenly right out of nowhere popped a sentry. He shouted the password and the Colonel the countersign, which, of all things, was the gag line of one of our most popular comic strips! (I thought: Of all things, at a time like this to play games!) This happened at regular intervals along the four-mile route, and every time it did, we almost choked to keep from laughing. So it wasn't such a bad idea.

Finally we began to enter what looked to be a town. The Colonel said, "This is Arzeu. The place I am taking you to is right in the heart of this town. Be on the alert, for snipers have been taking shots at us all evening."

He had hardly stopped speaking before: bang, bang, bang, bang. Four shots whistled by our heads, close enough for us to feel the breeze from them. My heart was going like a triphammer, and the Colonel said, "See what I mean?"

We saw all right, and, as one, the whole group sank down lower in the seat. We drove slowly along streets that were narrow and furtive, lined with palm trees that swayed in the breeze. Occasionally one could hear the echo of a shot from the other side of town and then a series of them, too near for comfort. Soon we turned into a short street, and I don't think the band on an M.P.'s arm ever looked so good to me as did the one a certain boy was wearing who stood guard outside what appeared to be a high fence enclosing some sort of compound. He shouted that silly little old password, a voice from inside the jeep gave the countersign, and the gate was opened just wide enough for us to walk through.

I was so stiff and cramped from being crowded in the jeep that I could hardly move. And so were the others. But when a sudden shot kicked up the dirt in front of us we moved, and fast!

It was discovered a little later that our friend who had greeted us so rudely was perched on a housetop across the street. Nice playful little fellow, I thought grimly.

"What sort of a place is this?" I now asked of no one in particular. From what I could see in the darkness, it appeared to be a rather square building about three stories high. A guard volunteered the information that it had been used by an old French midwife for an obstetrical home before the war.

As we reached the door, the guard shouted for them to extinguish their flashlights, that someone was coming in. We waited a second, then a blanket was pulled back — it had been rigged outside the door — and we stepped into the room.

The first thing that struck you were the odors. The unmistakable odor of filth and dirt, mixed with the odor of old blood and stale ether. There was a suppressed groan here and another there, and then a voice over in the corner: "May I have a drink of water? I've had nothing since three o'clock this morning." It was now nine-thirty, and the Lord only knew what the lad had been through in those hours!

One of the boys flashed on his light, and I shall never forget the sight that spread out before my eyes in that room. Rows upon rows of American boys lay on litters all over the floor. Just barely enough room to step over them to get around. There were pools of blood beside some of them, where dressings had not been changed since the first shock dressing was applied in the field. I don't know how the other girls felt, but I experienced at once a violent anger — bitter, surging anger — against a people that, out of greed and power and lust, would cause such things to happen to young manhood.

We found that we were to help in surgery with the boys who were most seriously wounded. The captain in charge of the group had one of the enlisted men take each of us through the building in an effort to weed these out and have them brought to the second floor, where a surgery of sorts had been set up. As we walked along, and the beam from the flashlight played over the faces of these boys, it was evident they were all in intense pain. But not a word of complaint was being uttered. Every mother with a son in this war, I thought grimly, could be proud of the sort of man he turns out to be under fire!

We climbed the moldy stairs to the second floor. It was very cold up there, as most of the windows had been blown out, and unlike the first floor all the openings were not covered with blankets. Rats were nosing about at will, but we hardly noticed them. As I straddled a litter to continue across the hall, a boy looked up at me and asked, "Please, is there any water anywhere? I'm terribly thirsty."

Now we had been told that the quart of water we had in our canteen was all we would get until a water point could be established. But what nurse could refuse such a request? Without a moment's hesitation, I bent down and, supporting the boy's head in my hand, helped him to drink from my canteen. As he dropped back onto the litter, gasping a little from pain, I asked, "Is that better, sonny? Where do you hurt?"

There was a moment's silence and then: "My God! A woman, an American woman! Where in heaven's name did you come from?" He was almost sobbing as he finished.

There has never been a time in my life that I have been so proud to be a nurse, to be able to help.

"Yes, sonny," I said. "An American woman, a nurse. And there are sixty of us from home over here to take care of you, get you well, so you'll be able to get back out there and beat the pants off the guy that got you — and hundreds like you."

I flashed the light down toward his face, shielding it with my hand from the open window. A boy about twenty, his face contorted with pain, his lips bleeding where he had bitten them to keep from crying out, but his eyes bright and unafraid. He had a bullet wound, grazing his groin — a horrible thing to look at. It had evidently been hurriedly covered with a shock dressing when the corpsmen brought him in, and then had not been changed owing to the number of casualties arriving so fast. There were bits of dirt, shreds from his trousers, all buried deep into the tissue of the soft part of his groin. It had evidently bled quite a lot at the time, and great clots of blood oozed out from around the dressing.

I indicated to the corpsman that here was one that we would do right away, and he and another boy picked up the litter and carried him to our improvised operating room. Then I finished my tour of the second floor, finding many cases to be handled at once, and passed on to the third. Here I ran into Kelly and Atkins, who had covered the ground before me. They stood talking together in low undertones.

Kelly, a girl in her middle thirties from Wilmington, Delaware, was saying, "I have worked in the accident room of a city hospital, and I've never seen anything to compare to the horrors I've seen within the last twenty minutes. We've surely got our work cut out for us." With this remark she started down the stairs.

Edna stood there a minute, seemingly unable to take in all that was happening to us. She was such a tiny thing, it almost seemed one should be taking care of her rather than she trying to do her bit to make it easier for the wounded. She looked at me for a second and then said, "Haskell, I had no idea it would be like this, did you?"

"No," I said. "I guess none of us realized what we were getting into. But we are here and we have a job to do. Perhaps the sooner we get to it, the better."

We linked arms and walked slowly down to the second floor. Just as we arrived there, Captain Borgemyer was rolling up his sleeves.

"Can any of you girls give ether?" he asked.

No one answered. Finally I said, "Well, I haven't given it for years, but I'm willing to if you're willing to have me."

With that, we all proceeded into the room we were to use for surgery. That room was something to behold. An improvised operating table in the center under a drop light with about a twenty-watt bulb in it (which, incidentally, burned out within the next few minutes), a small hand-basin and spigot. The water just dribbled from the spout, for the regular supply had been cut off by the French before we took over the town. A huge packing case for the anesthetist to use for a stool, one table, a small sterilizer that burned alcohol, a scalpel, a mere handful of clamps, and a pair of surgical scissors completed our equipment. It was positively heartbreaking when one thought of all the excellent equipment standing on board ship in the harbor.

The corpsmen found some flashlights, and we got ready to start the biggest night's work in our lives. Luckily the battalion aid field chest contained a fair quantity of alcohol and sutures, and plenty of ether and sulfa drugs. The doctors had rolled up their sleeves and were washing their hands in a basin of alcohol.

Gone were the elaborate gowns, masks, drapes, and towels that all nurses associate with surgery. The first boy brought in had a huge bayonet slash on the inner side of his left upper arm. When one flexed his elbow, the brachial muscle popped in and out of the slash as though it were supposed to do so. We cut the sleeve out of his shirt on that side and, so far as the patient was concerned, this constituted the preparation.

I remember asking him, "Have you ever taken ether, soldier?"

He answered that he hadn't.

I told him not to become panicky, to breathe naturally and soon he would be asleep. I'll never forget his huge brown eyes looking straight up at me when I covered them, and a small frightened voice saying, "Say, this arm will be O.K., won't it? I've a score to settle. Those dirty bastards got my buddy."

We assured him he would be fit as a fiddle in no time, and soon his deep breathing indicated he was under. A nod to Kelly and she passed Captain Borgemyer the pitifully few instruments we had to work with. Kelly had her G.I. flashlight fastened to the band of her slacks, and that was all the light she had to work with in doing her job of trying to keep sterility where the instruments were concerned. The corpsmen were holding flashlights with the beam trained on the incision, and I couldn't help remembering how many times surgeons I had worked with in hospitals at home had thrown well-regulated fits when the lighting system wasn't just to their liking.

Soon one of the dentists relieved me at the post of anesthetizing, as I found that my rather small hands became tired very quickly holding the jaws of those men. I joined Kelly and helped get together more sutures and drains, for supplies were dwindling fast.

Boy after boy was sent in, operated on, then sent back to bed on a litter on the floor. I relieved the dentist at intervals, and it was during one of these periods that I nearly lost my life. Edna, who had been circulating among the wounded on the floor below, giving hypodermics here and there to make the going easier, had just entered the operating room to ask a question of the doctor. By opening the door she had innocently created a draft, causing the blankets over the window to blow ever so slightly.

Bang!

Instinctively I ducked as a bullet whistled past me and ricocheted off the wall behind my back. Believe me or not, I could feel a breeze as the wretched tiling missed my head by inches!

There was a short interval of silence, broken by the oaths that sprang from every mouth in the room. Apparently a sniper in a tree outside the window had shot at the glimpse of light when the blanket moved.

I have never seen a more incensed group of men than those in that room at the time. This happened not once but again and again through the night. Finally there was the sound of two shots outside the building, a dull thud as of a body falling to earth, and a cry. Then we weren't troubled any more. I wouldn't have believed it possible to get so much positive exultation as I did over the death of that sniper.

At about 4:30 a.m. our last patient was carried out of the room. There were dozens of others who needed attention, but these were less urgent cases that could wait until we had daylight to aid us. We now started another tour of the house to check on the boys we had operated on. Many were in a weakened condition. Several flasks of plasma, our miracle worker, were administered, and soon the boys responded, as they invariably do when given this new lease on life.

The first and second floors seemed under control, and I wandered up to the third to look around. A rat the size of a rabbit scampered past me. Then I heard a low moaning from one corner and went over to investigate. The beam of my light picked up the face of a lad whose entire left cheek had been blown away. He had also suffered a fractured leg and wounds of the abdomen. I gave him a shot of morphine, did what I could to change the position of his leg, and passed on.

I was a little sick at what I had seen. Noticing a room off this hall which I had missed on my first trip to the floor, I opened the door and stepped in. Almost before the beam of my flashlight picked up the horrible sight before me, the odor of stale blood and death reached my nostrils. In this room, just lying on the floor and in the most grotesque positions possible, were approximately thirty dead bodies: Arabs, French soldiers, and a few of our own American boys.

It seemed that many patients brought to the hospital were dead on arrival. Because of the time element and the constant firing outside, they had been stored here tentatively — put out of sight to be taken care of properly in daylight. The body nearest the door was that of a French officer in all his glory and gold braid, bright scarlet coat, yes, and with his shiny high boots on. I couldn't help thinking: Well, fella, you died the way most real soldiers would have it — with your boots on.

I leaned against the jamb of the door for a second, too sick with the horror of it all to move. I had closed my eyes and was trying to get a grip on myself when I felt a hand on my arm. A startled young voice said, "Ma'am, come away from there. That isn't for a girl to see — certainly not after the night you've put in."

I gratefully allowed myself to be led away by one of the young corpsmen who had been working with me in the operating room. When we reached the second floor, I reported to the Captain about the condition of the boy upstairs. He went up at once to see him, only to find that I had simply made his passing a little easier. Afterward we all sat on the stairs awaiting daybreak, too tired to move and yet unable to sleep with the constant din from the guns outside.

I was leaning my head against the bannister of the stairs, trying to relax, when someone pulled it over against their knee. In this position I must have dozed for nearly twenty minutes when I was disturbed by a familiar voice.

"Come on, miss, there are several new casualties in from the St. Cloud area. Guess we are needed again."

I looked up into the face of the same little corpsman who had led me away from the harrowing sight in the third-floor room. I thought: God bless your little G.I. soul, I never saw you before and I shall probably never see you again, but your heart is in the right place.

As we walked along to the operating room, I smiled a little to think what my chief nurse would say when I told her I had slept with my head on an enlisted man's knee! It only goes to show that one doesn't have to be an officer to be a gentleman.

The next few hours were busy ones, and as daybreak finally arrived I began to wonder about the rest of the outfit, why some of them hadn't come to relieve us. Was it possible that gunfire had meant they were in trouble? Oh, so many thoughts ran through my head that I was dizzy.

Finally, about three o'clock in the afternoon, the rest of the outfit came in through the gates, and maybe we weren't glad to see them! They told tales of being sniped at on the way into town, and one M.P. arrived who told us that just about twenty minutes after our outfit had got off the beach in trucks, an Italian plane had come over and strafed the devil out of it.

Captain Henry Carney, a big genial Irishman from Boston, brought word that they had found temporary quarters for us in barracks that had formerly been the old French garrison. Twelve girls were quickly assigned to do the work that three of us had been doing through the night, and the rest of us started off. We were just outside the compound gates, walking single file and well dispersed, when we heard the drone of planes. We were much too tired to become excited. But all of a sudden Captain Carney began yelling and shouting for us to hurry and get down in the slit trench. In we rushed, Edna and I close together, and it was pretty well crowded, believe me. There was the unmistakable odor of human excrement, and we found out, much to our disgust, that the Arabs used this trench for a privy!

In the morning we lost no time in crawling out. I thought: Well, now I've really seen everything. (But how terribly wrong I was!) When we finally reached the garrison, which was enclosed with a high wire fence, I was so tired that I didn't think I would ever be able to move again as long as I lived.

Some of these barracks, which had evidently been used for officers' quarters, were partitioned off into small rooms. We were divided into groups of five girls each, and that was that. No cots, bedding rolls, or a blessed thing but the floor to sleep on. But even a floor can feel good. I spread out my overcoat, dropped down on it, and promptly fell asleep.

I don't know how long I had been lying thus, for the other girls had obligingly gotten up without disturbing me. But I do know I was awakened by the sound of firing close at hand. About the time I came out of my daze, the door burst open and in came Captains Hourican and Murphy — on hands and knees! It seems the snipers were shooting down into the compound, and naturally everyone was interested in getting under cover in a hurry.

Captain Murphy, about six feet two inches tall, looked exceedingly funny simply sitting there against the wall. I said, "Listen here, you two, don't you know this is a ladies' boudoir? Besides, I've been up all night. Get out of here and let me sleep."

With that they apologized prettily and left, but in a much more dignified manner than they had arrived.

Presently the door opened again, and in staggered Miller with her arms full of some sort of olive drab material. "What in the name of heaven have you there?" I asked, mystified.

She puffed and panted a little and said, "Capes, French capes, soldiers' capes. There's a whole warehouse full of them, and I figured they'd make good bedding. I brought one for each of us." She smiled her winsome little smile and added, "You made it, didn't you, Yankee?"

I laughed a little and replied, "Yes, Rebel. I guess only the good die young and I'm going to live to a ripe old age."

I could laugh now, but last night it had been a different matter. I had been both thrilled and frightened, and as I thought it over I came to the conclusion that I wouldn't have missed it for anything — even the horrible parts of it.

Soon Miss Salter, our chief nurse, arrived on the scene looking worried. "What's the matter?" I asked. "Something wrong?"

"I've been thinking about night duty," she said. "I don't know who to put on. You know, we have patients over here in some of these buildings, now, too!"

I felt fairly decent from five hours' sleep, so I said, "If it will help any, I'll try another trick."

At first she wouldn't hear of it, remembering I had worked about eighteen hours the first stretch. But I kept at her stubbornly until she finally let me go on.

At seven o'clock I arrived on the ward, if you could call it that. There I found a group of twenty-seven boys. Some were able to get around, others were more seriously wounded. One lad confided, "Nurse, you know if a cow walked through here I could bite my steak right off the flank. I'm that hungry!" This brought a howl from the others, but it didn't alter the fact that many of them, myself included, felt pretty much the same way.

As yet, supplies had not been unloaded from the ship, and there was little in the way of food. I had some ration bars in my musette bag: concentrated chocolate. I knew there wasn't enough to go around, so I began to wonder what to do with what I had. I mused more to myself than to anybody else: "If I had some water, I could make hot chocolate."

Immediately there was a chorus of voices: "Hot chocolate! Oh, boy."

I thought: Haskell, think fast. These kids are hungry and they want hot chocolate. It's up to you to see they get it.

I walked back to the nurses' quarters and asked, "Who has a canteen full of water?" When I told them what I wanted it for, the girls came through in fine style. I returned to the ward with five canteens besides my own. We proceeded to make hot chocolate over the little alcohol burner of the sterilizer in the canteen cups. The look of contentment on the faces of those kids was worth the three burned fingers I had acquired!

Young James Marshbanks of Cincinnati, Ohio, was corporal of the guard that night and a wee bit nervous at that. He kept coming into the ward to see if we were all right, but I suspect he also wanted his own morale lifted. He said, "Remember, Miss Haskell, if they start firing, get down to the floor, fast."

I laughed and said, "Corporal, if they start in firing, I'm more than apt to go right through the floor. I've been fired on all that I want to be for a time."

This brought a series of questions from the patients. "Do you mean to tell us they fired on women?" "The dirty so-and-so's, I'd like to get my hands on them for about five minutes." "What kind of war is this, that they don't respect the medical corps? Damn their hides." If it does any good to get an army mad before it fights, I could see that these boys would do a good job once they got back to duty.

Within the next few days hostilities finally ceased, and we began working side by side with the people we had been fighting. Such is the way of war! A night or two later one of the M.P.'s rode through the gate in a hurry and shouted, "There's been a destroyer sunk in the harbor and they're bringing the casualties here. Have you room for them? They're English!"

"We certainly have," said our CO. promptly. "Bring them right in."

Soon an ambulance rolled up and a young English sailor was brought in on a stretcher. He was badly burned from steam, but it hadn't dampened his spirits.

"Lor', lydy, but it's cold in that there water," he stammered as he attempted to clasp his arms to warm himself. A grimace of pain crossed his face, and he dropped his hands to his sides once again.

There were several others, none of them too badly disabled. But they didn't seem to know what had happened, and told fantastic tales of how the bow of the ship suddenly rose out of the water, shuddered, and started down.

Soon our mess sergeant came in bearing huge pots of coffee — just the thing to warm them. But can you imagine it? They beefed because it wasn't teal English to the end, even in face of disaster.

We were operating two hospitals now, but most of it was routine work. Our casualties from the invasion were slowly getting better, and the work, after all the excitement, was a trifle boring. Most of the talk now had an entomological flavor. One morning a girl from one of the other hospitals drew me aside and said, "Are you having much trouble with roaches? The place down there is alive with them — three and four inches long."

"We aren't having roaches," I said. "But our bedbugs have us well under control."

I wasn't joking. In the end we had to retreat into the open. In other words: into tents, with fourteen girls assigned to each. I'd never lived out of doors in December, and I wasn't quite sure I would like it. Between bedbugs and cold, however, most of us were forced to the same preference. It was better to shiver than to scratch.

"Isn't it a pity," said Edna one very cold night when our teeth began chattering in unison. "They say the people in the States are virtually freezing on a lousy sixty-five degrees."

"What's the world coming to," I said. "Maybe we should send them some of this fine African heat."

December, ordinarily, meant thoughts about Christmas. But I didn't dare to think of it now. One afternoon, unexpectedly, a truck rolled in, and as it passed our tent, the boy on the back yelled "Mail!"

Mail, after all those weeks of not hearing from home! We all made headquarters in nothing flat, only to be told that the Chaplain would sort and distribute it after chow.

At chow that night every one of us was in rare good spirits, knowing — or at least hoping — there would be a letter in all the lot that had come. As I went back to my ward to await delivery of the mail, and make a last-minute check on the patients before the night nurse came, one of the boys who was walking with crutches smiled rather pathetically and said, "Nurse, if you get some of that mail and it isn't too personal, may I read it? I haven't had a letter in eight months."

I almost cried as I said, "You sure may."

Sergeant Michael Gregory walked through the door with both hands full of letters fanned out like cards. I prayed: Dear Lord, let one of them be for me, just one, that's all I ask!

Mike, as the boys called him, came forward and said to the patients, "Boys, how has she been treating you?"

The gang all shouted, "O.K."

He laughed and, coming up to me, said, "They are all yours, twenty-eight of them. And the one on top is from your son!"

Bless him, he knew the one I had been praying for! I crept off into the corner to read them and to have my little private cry, and I couldn't remember when I had been so happy. One of them was from a girl friend with a rare sense of humor, and since her letter was full of nonsense as usual, I looked up the crippled soldier who hadn't had any mail in eight months. As I left to go to my tent to rest, I looked back to see his face wreathed in smiles. Why, oh why, I thought to myself sadly, won't the folks back home be more considerate? There is more than one method of being "under fire." Men can stand the actual battles, but the endless waiting for word from home is twice as hard!

Rumor had it we were going to move again. I wondered where. Eastward, in all probability. If so, I was hoping it would be soon. From what we had been hearing, our boys over there could use our help. December, Christmas, peace on earth, good will to men! Oh, Lord, might we not soon again be a world united instead of a world at each other's throats!

CHAPTER EIGHT: Holiday Season in a Strange Country

I HAD SPENT several Christmases away from my home during my nursing career but none that could compare with the one I spent in Arzeu, Algeria, in 1942.

I was making the rounds with our chief nurse on the morning of the nineteenth of December. The fighting now was much farther away, the guns had stopped rumbling, and there were moments occasionally when we could think of other things. Suddenly she turned to me and said:

"Lieutenant Haskell, I have news for the girls. It seems there are fifteen mail bags for the outfit at the base post office in Oran. The CO. is sending in a detail of our enlisted men this afternoon to help sort it in time for Christmas. Isn't that grand?"

At the mention of Christmas you could see the faces of our young patients fall and a faraway look come into their eyes. One could stand being homesick at any time of year better than at the Christmas season. I began to wonder just what we were to do about it.

Genevieve Kruszic got the first really brilliant idea that evening. "Ruth, would you do something for me?" she asked, drawing me aside.

"Surely, if I can," I replied.

"I want the girls to do a little sewing for me. We're going to make Christmas stockings for the patients. If each girl will sew on them, we'll get them done in time. The Red Cross director was here from Oran today, and if we'll make them, they'll get something to put into them by Christmas morning. I think it's a cute idea, don't you?"

"It's an excellent idea," I agreed. "I know the other girls will think so, too. Most of us have needle and thread tucked away in our belongings."

Just then Vaughn Fisher came along, smiling and humming to herself.

"You sound mighty happy, young lady. What's cooking?" I asked.

"We're going to have a Christmas tree for the boys over at our unit. Are you folks going to have one, too?"

"You bet we are," I said, aware of it for the first time. I thought: If they can manage, certainly we can, too.

As the conversation lagged, I left the tent in search of Captain Forman, our special services officer, to find out if there was to be anything done about a tree for our patients. I found him over by his tent scrubbing away at his mess kit, which he had burned in an amateurish attempt to fry one lonely little egg he had acquired from an Arab in exchange for a package of gum.

"Captain," I said, "what are we going to do about a Christmas tree for the patients? Second Unit has one, and I think we should have one, too. Lieutenant Kruszic is in charge of having some stockings made, but I feel we should do more if we can. Some of these boys are away from home for the first time in their lives. This week has been pretty terrible for them, and next week will be worse."

"I have a detail of boys taking care of it," he assured me. "I'm planning to set it up outside so the ambulatory patients can help decorate it too. Goodness knows what we'll do for decorations, but at least Utilities will have a few lights we can use for a while on Christmas Eve."

I went back to my tent feeling much better about the outlook. As I walked along I wondered what we could do to decorate our barnlike ward so that the boys who were unable to get out of bed might have their morale lifted, too. I decided to talk it over with Mary Meyer, who worked on the ward with me and who also lived in my tent.

That night I beckoned to her to come down from her upper bunk and sit on my cot and have a cigarette with me.

"What is it, Ruth?" she asked. "Has something happened?" This was always the logical question.

"Mary," I said, "have you given any thought to instilling the ward with Christmas spirit?"

She thought for a minute, and her attractive face was a study. Soon a smile wreathed over it, and she brushed her blonde hair back from her eyes and said,

"We could sing, couldn't we? Everybody loves carols, and most of the boys like to sing anyway. For that matter, we don't have to wait until Christmas Eve. How about starting tonight?"

We received permission from the Chief Nurse, and the hour was arranged. When we arrived in the ward we found a rather morose-looking group of boys. But they soon became interested when Mary walked down the center of the room and, smiling glamorously, announced:

"Come on, boys, we are going to sing carols. Remember? I'm sure that most of you know them, but if you don't know the words, you can hum."

The boys looked askance at each other, and for the first song or two Mary and I were really doing a duet. She could actually sing, but I wasn't anything to write home about. Presently a boy's voice joined in, then another and another, from different parts of the room, until finally every last one of them was singing. We ran through one carol after another, then drifted off into "My Wild Irish Rose," "Sidewalks of New York," "I've Been Working on the Railroad," and "The Girl on the Flying Trapeze." It was amazing what a few songs and a little laughter could do for the morale of these boys. Let no one doubt that a man's spirit needs as much care and attention as his physical hurts. When we rose to leave, there were cries of "Don't go yet, it's early." We told them we'd do it again, and went away, leaving behind us a smiling, happy group of faces in place of the sad ones that had received us.

As we stepped out into the night, it was clear and cold and bright moonlight.

"Oh, Ruthie, look. Isn't it gorgeous? Wouldn't it be swell sitting out somewhere in a quiet park back home with a man's arms around us?"

"Two men's arms around us," I corrected. But I knew what she was thinking. Lonesome for a man, with men all over the landscape — busy at something else. Some of those little G.I.'s were darned nice kids, but this was the army, Mr. Jones, and I suppose the regulation regarding our being on a friendly basis with them was necessary or they wouldn't have made it.

As we went to the chow line next day at noon, we came upon a group of our enlisted men setting up the most straggly-looking evergreen I ever saw. It seemed they had gone twelve miles out from the area in search of a tree, and this was the best they could find. From where I stood, it looked like a Maypole, and some of the patients who were able to get about stood around it in groups, evidently discussing what could be done with it. The boys on the detail had managed to collect some trailing evergreen somewhere, but we didn't get up much enthusiasm until we had eaten our lunch and returned to the ward to finish the day.

"I wonder what can be done with that tree out there?" Mary asked.

"Goodness, I wouldn't know," I replied. "We already have a flagpole."

"What tree?" asked one of the boys.

I explained that an "alleged" evergreen tree had been set up out in the court. "Maybe it will end up as a Christmas tree, but right now I wouldn't bet on it."

"Maybe you have some ideas," suggested Mary, giving the soldier a playful wink.

This particular boy, I knew, did have ideas aplenty. He was from one of the armored regiments, and his very first idea upon landing was to go A.W.O.L. and get befuddled on African wine. He was still entrenched in the doghouse so far as the CO. was concerned. But he grinned good-naturedly, gave Mary a friendly pat on one shoulder, and went out to where the tree was standing. He didn't come back for some time, so I sent one of the corpsmen out to see what had become of him. When the corpsman didn't return either, I put on my cape and went out to hunt for them.

I found them both over by the tree, busily engaged in cutting decorations out of ration cans with the tin snips they had borrowed from Utilities! They had stars and disks and all sorts of whirligigs. My friend with ideas seemed to be enjoying himself. And not on African' wine.

The next day all the mail from Oran arrived by truck, and I think everybody in the unit had several letters and packages. Most of us couldn't wait for Christmas to come, we were so curious about our packages, so that night we had a real spree and opened most of them. I'm sure if our parents and friends could have seen the expressions on our faces when we examined the contents, they would have laughed, too. They had been used to giving us things we could use at home, and here we were hundreds of miles away, living in tents and coveralls and men's shoes, and the things some of those packages contained! White silk hose and white slips, for us who had not worn dresses in weeks. One of the girls got a very pretty bed jacket, which, incidentally, she gave to me when I became a patient weeks later — so at least we got some good out of that! There were bottles of perfume, and cosmetics, and books. Also candy and fruitcakes which we nearly died eating. A friend of mine who knew me rather well sent two beautiful lipsticks, and did I welcome them! As I had once told my CO., if ever I should stop using make-up there would be nothing left of my morale. A fresh application of lipstick, my helmet at a jaunty angle, and I was ready for anything. Luckily my parents had sent me two pair of warm pajamas and a pair of slacks, and not before I needed them, either.

The next day, on duty, I found Mary and our young soldier in deep conversation, and I naturally suspected mischief. I heard Mary say,

"All right, we'll go and get them on my off-duty hours."

"You'll go where to get what?" I asked, knowing at least one of Mary's weaknesses.

"Never you mind, we have something up our sleeves and we'll tell you when we are finished," she replied.

"Yeah man," chimed in the soldier.

It soon came time for her to leave, and she and the boy started off toward town, a couple of blocks away. When next I saw them again, they were carrying parcels and talking with great animation.

"What have you there?" I asked as they came into the ward.

"Oh, Ruthie, we're going to have decorations for the ward after all. We saw these little figurines downtown this morning, and we are going to make a crib with the Nativity represented by these tiny figures. Aren't they cute?"

As she was talking, she unwrapped her packages, and the little figures were indeed lovely. The Christ Child, Mary and Joseph and the wise men, some tiny little sheep, and a manger. They were all there and beautifully painted.

"Where on earth did you find them?" I asked, my respect for our soldier friend increasing.

"I found them," said he, "in a small shop off the public square. They weren't very expensive. There were more of them at one time, but the Germans carried them off before the invasion."

Mary sent him over to Utilities, and the boys there built him a small crib, and when he came back we squandered enough cotton to pad it. He arranged it in the center of the ward so it could be seen from nearly every angle. Then he put the light down behind it after covering the bulb with a piece of red cloth from our Christmas stocking material. This shed a red glow upon the small figures, and it was really beautiful. Nearly everyone came to the ward to see it during the few remaining days before Christmas. I remember our chaplain saying that the boy couldn't be so very bad when he could create such a beautiful thing. Some of the other boys then became interested and made a wreath of sorts out of the trailing evergreen and tied a piece of the red cloth to it to hang on the outside of the door. I wonder what the soldiers from that French garrison would have said if they could have seen the varied uses we made of their gay red sashes.

While we were admiring this unusual creation, Louise Miller nudged me and said, "Ruth, Carl says he thinks you and I and he and Rob can get into Oran for dinner Christmas Eve. Jane Ferree and Lieutenant Greenleaf may join us too. Won't that be fun?"

The outlook grew brighter and brighter. When Christmas Eve arrived, I was agog with excitement. "Maybe we'll dance at the Chantilly Club, too," I ventured. "I'm just crazy to dance once again." Somehow we hadn't thought much of playing, the past few weeks. But now our men were convalescing, the military situation was reported to be improving, and we were, after all, only human.

Carl, Rob, and Lieutenant Greenleaf were friends of ours from the signal corps group there in Arzeu who had come from the States to England on the same ship with us. The six of us had enjoyed a pleasant friendship. As for the Chantilly Club, it was operated by the Army in Oran to give the officers and nurses a place to go for relaxation. It was a typical night club, but the thing that made it different was the fact that it opened at seven and closed at ten-thirty! Oran was off limits to the military personnel after that hour, and we had to be off the streets or take the chance of being picked up by the M.P.'s.

In the afternoon Rob had to go into town on business, so he stopped by the hospital to tell me they would be by for us at seven. This was just before chow time. When I hit the chow line with my mess kit at four-forty-five, everybody was crowded around the bulletin board talking excitedly.

"What's wrong?" I asked when I got within speaking distance.

"Oh, Ruth, we are alerted," wailed Louise. "That means we must stay on the compound. Isn't that awful?"

"Why are we alerted?" I asked, feeling suddenly very low.

"Come look at this," Louise said, leading me to the bulletin board. It read that due to the assassination of Admiral Darlan in Algiers all units of the American military would be alerted and must remain on their posts until further notice.

I suppose we should have been chiefly concerned about Darlan, but truthfully, the thing that seemed to jar everyone at the moment was the fact that we couldn't leave the compound. Christmas Eve of all nights, to have to stay on the post!

The Commanding Officer must have sensed our tobogganing morale, for he addressed us appealingly:

"I'm very sorry about this alert, for I realize some of you had plans for the evening. Fact is, I did myself, but it's one of those things you must accept when you're in the Army. We're going to have the victrola and records in the mess hall this evening, and those who want to can come there to dance. Perhaps it will be a poor substitute for what you might have planned, but let's make the best of a bad situation and be good soldiers."

Soon it began to rain, the same slow drizzle we had been having at intervals for days. I swear that everything that I owned was covered with mud in one form or another. Huge clouds completely shut off the starlight. I was sitting on a packing box in the shadow of the tent, indulging in a little self-pity I guess, when the Chaplain arrived. He sat down beside me for a minute, and I continued to sniffle into my handkerchief.

"Don't cry, Ruth, I know you are disappointed," he said gently. "I've been talking to Miller, and she's all upset, too. Do you realize that, for the first time in your life, and perhaps for the only time in your life, you are in a setting comparable with that of the first Christmas? That Arab and his sheep on the hillside across the way might easily have been one of the wise men. You have much to be thankful for. You are well, you've weathered two hazardous ocean trips, and you have the love and respect of your patients and friends. All in all, you are a fortunate girl. That small son of yours is another thing to be thankful for. Many women live and die and never know the joy and pain of motherhood. No one can take that from you. Come on now, get those shoulders back. It isn't like you to let anything get you down so far. Least of all something over which you've no control. Chin up, girl!"

As he finished speaking, the clouds actually lifted, and a full moon lighted up the landscape. From the engineers' area adjacent to us came the muted sounds of a trumpet playing "Silent Night, Holy Night." As he played, silent figures began emerging from the tents to listen.

We were all so intent on the beautiful rendition of one of our favorite carols that we hadn't heard the rest of the band come in at the gate and assemble in the court before the tree. As the last strains of "Silent Night" faded in the moonlight, the band started playing "Oh, Little Town of Bethlehem." They continued with other familiar carols, and before they finished, all the patients who could walk were outside the ward listening. They finished their impromptu program with "God Bless America"; and as I looked around in the bright moonlight at the upturned faces of those young soldiers, the thought went through my mind that ours was indeed a cause worth fighting for.

As the boys went back to their wards, many of them leaning on the arms of their buddies, they all stopped in front of the tree. Some were on crutches, others walked with canes, and still others had arms and legs in casts. As each turned away from the tree, blinking to keep back the tears they feared it would be unmanly to let fall, you knew that they, too, were remembering other Christmas Eves, when they had had their families, wives, or sweethearts with them. Needless to say, I no longer felt so miserably alone.

The Catholic chaplain with the second unit held a midnight mass, from which many of us derived a great deal of comfort. The altar was beautifully decorated and the mass well attended. Catholics and Protestants alike attended, with no thought of differences of creed.

Christmas morning at last arrived, and for once the sun shone brightly. That was a help in itself. The Red Cross had filled the stockings we girls had made, and each boy had two candy bars, two packs of cigarettes, a pack of cards, a comb, and a handkerchief. They were all very grateful and tried hard to show us their appreciation.

Somehow, walking out of the ward that morning made me realize how lucky I was just to be whole.

With Christmas over, we set about removing the decorations from the ward. There seemed now to be less tension about the place. I think we had all secretly dreaded the holiday and were secretly glad that it was over.

"Girls," said the Chief Nurse next day, "you must repack your bedding rolls. Colonel Ringer says they are entirely too big. We are to move on again very soon, and no girl's roll should exceed eighteen inches in diameter. That means you must either send some things home or give them to the natives who have been doing your laundry. When we move, we are going in train convoy, and there will be only one baggage car for the bedding rolls of both officers and nurses. So see what you can do about them."

As she finished speaking, we all groaned and began to chatter about the rolls. When we had left England, we had been obliged to leave our foot lockers in storage there, just outside London, and had of course transferred as much of our belongings to our bedding rolls as possible. Mine was a huge affair, as were most of the others. The worst of it was when we got at the job of repacking them. Every time one girl would throw something out, another would grab it and put it into hers! So all in all we just shuffled most of the stuff around. Later, when we got out into the field to live, it was amusing to hear one girl wail about something she thought she had thrown away, only to have another girl produce it for her.

"Lieutenant Haskell, you are wanted on the telephone down in headquarters." This from one of the enlisted men in the office. He was looking at me as though I were something out of fiction, because we weren't allowed to use the phone at headquarters.

I hurried to the phone, feeling suddenly very important. "Lieutenant Haskell speaking," I said, with plenty of curiosity.

"Hello," said Rob's voice. "I guess I am a little late, but Merry Christmas. I was O.D. yesterday and couldn't find a minute to call you. It's only with the kind permission of my company commander that I'm able to now. How have you been?"

Needless to say, I was thrilled to death to receive what would have been an ordinary phone call at home but what was really an event here. A little later Carl called Louise. That was their contribution to our holiday spirit, and believe me, it surely helped. We really were the envy of the other girls, who hadn't received a phone call in the many weeks since we had left England.

Within the next day or two a notice appeared on our bulletin board to the effect that an infantry regiment was going to give a New Year's party and that all of the nurses of our unit were cordially invited. It also said we would be called for in trucks and delivered safely home at the close of the party. We all began to hope that the alert, which was still effective, would be lifted in time, for that could well be our very last party before getting up into the zone of combat.

When Lieutenant Salter made rounds on the ward the morning of the thirty-first, she told me:

"Lieutenant Haskell, I think you girls can count on going to the party tonight. The Colonel thinks the alert will be lifted sometime today, judging from a message he has received. If it is, a couple of the girls who don't dance will relieve the night nurses who do. I want to let as many as possible go to this affair, because it will be the last in some time to come. You've been good girls and you deserve a little fun. Keep your fingers crossed, and we'll hope the alert will be off by late afternoon."

Sure enough, when we went to chow at the supper hour there was the notice on the board that the alert was lifted and we could leave the compound. Such brushing of clothes you never did see. We hadn't worn our uniforms in weeks, and they were a sorry-looking sight, to say nothing of our shirts, which were crisscrossed with wrinkles! We may have not looked so well, but we sure smelled good when we left that evening. Most of us had received perfume or cologne of some sort for Christmas, and we certainly poured it on for the boys of the infantry. Many of the girls had shampooed and brushed their hair until it shone. All in all, maybe we didn't look too bad.

"Come on now, Haskell," said Edna, "the trucks are here and Lieutenant Salter is waiting. Let's get going before they decide to have another alert."

"Come on, gal!" sang out Vaughn as she reached down a hand to help me into the back of the big old army truck.

"Oh, Lordy," I gasped as I swung myself up. For a minute I could hardly straighten, the pain down the small of my back was so severe.

"Good heavens I Whatever is the matter?" she asked anxiously.

"Nothing at all now," I answered. I didn't want to say any more about it, because Lieutenant Salter had got into the truck directly behind me and I didn't want her to tell me I had to go on sick call. Things were just about to get under way, what with our move in the offing, and I didn't intend to miss anything if I could help it.

When we went into the theater where the boys were having their party, I forgot my aching back entirely. The seats in the theater were of the removable type, and the boys had the place set up in cabaret style. There were huge cactus leaves with G.I. candles for centerpieces, and it was all very lovely to look at. There was a Christmas tree, too, which showed much ingenuity on the part of whoever had dressed it. The music was good, and the boys were friendly and courteous. We saw the New Year in with a drink of champagne and got properly kissed in the bargain. All too soon it came time to leave, and I wondered, as we bumped and jostled along the way home, just what the New Year would bring.

"You are to go to the mess hall for an issue of C rations directly after chow," said the Chief Nurse next morning as she stood before us thumbing through some papers she held in her hand. "It looks as though it won't be too long now before we start moving. You girls who are in charge of wards, make out a list of your patients today. On this list we want all the pertinent information regarding the patients. But mostly we want to know the name, serial number, organization, and diagnosis. All the patients in the hospital are to be evacuated within the next three days, so be sure their records are in order." She smiled shyly and then added: "You know, I don't like C rations any better than you do, but I've come to the conclusion they are better than nothing."

We went to the mess sergeant for our issue, sputtering all the time about canned rations. If we had realized how long we were destined to exist on the things, we probably would have done more than sputter. The food was perfectly adequate, but it was the monotony that got you down. Meat and beans, hash, and then more meat and beans, with an occasional bit of Spam and corned beef thrown in for good measure. Not a thing wrong with it as a food, but just so darned tiresome!

Within the next few days we got all our patients' records in order and had them catalogued for reference. The day they moved out, headed for the various general and station hospitals that had been set up in the area since our arrival, we were actually sorry to see them go. A good many of them had been with us for the entire two months of our stay at Arzeu. They had been hurt early in the invasion and had spent their entire convalescing period with us, and we had come to be old friends.

We spent a couple of days resting and getting packed. Many of us went into Oran with the supply truck that last evening for one final dinner and fling before abandoning our uniforms for coveralls for the winter.

The Commanding Officer posted a notice that we were to meet with him at noon on the day of our scheduled departure.

"Members of this command," he began in his most dignified voice. "You are to be commended for the way you behaved under fire and for the excellent work you did with the casualties following the invasion. The first step of our trip is behind us, and the most hazardous lies just ahead. We leave here by truck convoy at midnight. At Oran we board a train carrying troops into the combat zone. From there on in we'll be on the spot. We can only hope that our luck holds as well as it has thus far. I am proud of you as a group, and I know you will continue to give me the same good co-operation you have given up to now. Good luck to you, and may God be with us!"

We were on the move again.

CHAPTER NINE: On the Move Once Again

"Help me tighten the straps on this bedding roll, will you, Ruthie?" panted Louise as she stood straddle of the thing trying to hold it closed with her knees. "I've tugged and tugged, and every time I let go with my knees, the darned thing unrolls again!"

"Be right there, honey, I've troubles of my own," I said. One thing I was sure of was that if I ever reached the States again I'd never go on another camping trip, nor even on a picnic. It would be white linen table cloths and real silver or nothing.

At that minute the door of the barracks opened and First Sergeant Gregory announced that we must have our baggage ready for the detail of enlisted men to pick up in half an hour. We groaned and shouted some rather uncomplimentary remarks, then set to work with a vengeance.

While we were struggling with the straps, the Chief Nurse bounced in to remind us we were to be in the trucks and ready to leave at exactly midnight, which was not too far away. Although it hadn't seemed possible, we were actually packed and sitting patiently (?) on our bedding rolls when the boys arrived to pick them up. We did our usual amount of heckling as they tightened the straps still farther and threw them up into the trucks, and they were very audible in their comments about our having a piano in each one.

"Come on now, let's get this show on the road," roared the Sergeant as we filed along beside the trucks.

"Remember your blood pressure, Sergeant," said Edna. "Don't you know you'll never reach old age if you get excited like that?"

He grinned a little and began to hand us into the trucks. The weight of the equipment had been getting mighty heavy, and I, for one, was grateful for a chance to sit down. Then, too, it was good to be on our way. The work had been so light and routine that we were all anxious to get up to where they needed us badly.

As we began to pull out of town, the blackout lights on the trucks could pick up the swarthy faces of many of our Arab friends standing beside the road, bewildered by all this sudden activity after the weeks of comparative quiet which had followed the invasion. Many of them grinned toothlessly and lifted their hands in the V sign for victory that they had picked up from us. I wondered how they would get along after we left, and if another outfit would move in to adopt them.

"Let's sing," said Mary.

"Why don't you settle for some sleep?" asked Lieutenant Don Macintosh. "You're about the singingest female I've ever seen."

Mary grinned in the semidarkness. "Maybe so, but if you go to sleep in this thing when we hit that stretch of road at St. Cloud, you'll break your crazy neck, so let's sing to keep from doing just that."

A few of us began to hum, and then others joined in. I couldn't help thinking that here we were starting out for the Lord only knew where, and as unconcerned as if we were going for a joy ride back home. (I'll still vote for the Americans and the way they take things in their stride when under stress!) In just a few minutes the city of Oran began to loom up in the darkness. We quieted down and rode through town easily and without much ado. Soon we rolled down into the railroad yard and went aboard the trains from the freight section. This time we were assigned six girls to a compartment, and before long we were grateful that we weren't as crowded as we had been on the last train trip. My compartment-mates were Louise, Millie Harris, Margaret Hornback, "Sherry" Sheridan, and a girl whom we called Teddy because her last name was Baer. We quickly arranged our equipment in the most practical manner and then began to discuss what we would do about trying to get comfortable. I was for getting a little sleep.

"It has just occurred to me," ventured Hornback, "that two of us can sleep on the floor between the seats and then the other four can curl up on the seats, two to a side with their heads in the corner and their feet and legs passing each other. How does that sound to the rest of you?"

"I'll take the floor if you don't mind," I put in quickly. I knew I could be straighter there than on the seat, and I still had trouble with my back.

"O.K., I'll sleep there with you," said Louise. "We can use one overcoat for a blanket and the other for a mattress." That was putting it euphemistically.

Millie Harris had been inspecting the seats while we were talking, and she looked up and said,

"Come here a minute, Haskell. Don't you think we could take these cushions off the seats and put them on the floor for you two? There are felt-covered springs under them, and with our coats around us we can do very nicely on the seats, and the cushions would take up a little of the shock and vibration for you on the floor."

"Grand idea," I said. "Remind me to kiss you sometime." We put the cushions on the floor and tried to get settled before the cattle car got under way. We soon were nicely tucked in, and when the Colonel and the Chief made their check just a short while later they were greatly amused, because part of the girls were still milling around trying to get settled and the rest of us were at least pretending to be asleep.

I lay awake a long time after the other girls, looking out the window of the car and wondering just how much would happen to us before we were in a city the size of Oran again. About an hour after we had boarded the train, it began to rattle slowly out of town, and soon the sound of the wheels on the tracks and the vibration of the car itself lulled me into a troubled sleep. It had become very cold, and the floor of that train was as hard as any floor I had yet slept on in Africa. The next time I wakened, the sun was high in the heavens and Millie Harris was sitting up looking out of the window. When she noticed I was awake, she smiled rather winsomely and said,

"I've been watching out of the windows since daybreak. This is certainly beautiful country, but it goes by in slow motion. I swear I could walk faster than this train is traveling."

"I'd just as soon not try it," I said sleepily. When at last I struggled to a sitting position, I noticed we were climbing steadily into the hill country. On the right side of the tracks were sheer plateaus, stretching out for miles; and the way the sun was casting light and shadows, it seemed that every color of the rainbow was spread out before us. Not too far away were several Arabs with their herds of sheep and goats, and one in particular reminded me of Joseph, in the Bible, with his coat of many colors. More and more I was beginning to connect scenes and people in this type of country with the stories in the Bible.

As I started to speak to Millie about the beauty all around us, there was a knock on the door of the compartment and then the voice of Lieutenant Macintosh.

"Everybody up! We are going to stop in a very few minutes, and then the boys from the kitchen car will be through with some breakfast. Stay in your compartments and we'll serve you there. It will make for less confusion than if everyone crowded into these narrow aisles."

"How did you sleep?" I asked.

"Personally," said the Lieutenant, "I felt better before I tried to rest."

"You certainly wouldn't take any beauty prize with that beard you have, either!" commented Louise saucily.

"Why, you brat!" The Lieutenant shook his fist at her menacingly. "Just for that, you'll go without breakfast. Just wait and see if you don't."

At that she wailed and apologized prettily, and the Lieutenant went off grinning and whistling.

She and I struggled to our feet and put the cushions back onto the seats. All in all we hadn't done too badly, and I was agreeably surprised to find that my muscles still worked when I tried them. I suppose one can get used to sleeping on floors, even cold ones.

Soon the boys from the kitchen came through with hot oatmeal, fried eggs (powdered, of course), hardtack, and coffee. This, followed by the usual cigarette, left us quite at peace with the world for the time being.

"Man, oh, man, but I'm glad we have our kitchen car," said Hornback. "Imagine existing on cold C rations while on a train like this one."

"Imagine trying to exist on C rations anywhere," somebody piped up playfully.

"What about cleaning our mess kits?" asked Sherry. "There is only cold water in the cans for drinking, and I don't imagine that the Colonel would appreciate our washing our dishes in that."

"What say we hop down off this train and stretch our legs," said Teddy. "Then, if they get angry, they can send us back to the States."

It developed that we got permission to leave the train while the engineer fetched water for the engine.

"Girls, bring your mess kits with you and we can wash them in the steam from the engine."

We looked around to see where this bright thought came from, and we discovered the Chaplain practicing what he preached. His mess kit came out just as clean and shining, and in a very few minutes we were a long line waiting to do the same thing. As we stood there, the natives — for there were always natives — began crowding around us, holding forth tangerines and honest-to-goodness eggs. Soon the usual bartering began, in the course of which most of us came off with some fruit and two or three eggs in exchange for a pack or two of cigarettes. The strange part of it was, these people didn't want money, only candy, gum, or cigarettes. Those of us who had eggs marked them with a pencil and gave them to Sergeant Roberts, who took them to the kitchen car and boiled them for us in the water in which he made our coffee. (An ingenious man, obviously.) They certainly tasted good, because we had only two meals a day and most of us could have eaten ten.

"Ruth, look over here," Louise said. "A cotton field!"

"Imagine it," I said. "After spending over a year in our own beloved South, I have to come to North Africa to see a cotton field!"

This made the others laugh, for every last one of them in my compartment was a Rebel.

"Think nothing of it, honey," one of them said. "I went down to Maine once, and sure enough I didn't see any potatoes growing."

The day passed slowly in small talk such as this, and many of the members of the outfit whiled away the time playing solitaire, readying their equipment, reading, or singing in small groups here and there. Also, as was inevitable in a group of professionals, we heard tall tales of training days among the nurses and internships among the men. When night came on once again I held out stubbornly for the floor, though there were in the compartment those who now suspected I was getting the long end of the bargain.

The next day passed uneventfully, with the train stopping every eight or ten miles to refuel or get water. It was a steady uphill grind, and we made slow progress. I had been dozing in the sunlight that was streaming through the window when I wakened suddenly and glanced out at the mountains. I couldn't believe my eyes.

"Look up there! It's snowing," I gasped. "Snow, in Africa, of all places!" I had always pictured Africa as being a tropical kind of country with jungles and snakes and things. And now I had seen a cotton field and snow — both within forty-eight hours. Would wonders never cease?

"I don't see anything to get excited about," said Sherry. "It just looks darned cold to me." The others agreed with her that it did to them, too, so I went in search of someone who could enjoy the sight as I did. Fact was, it made me a little homesick, because here it was the middle of the winter and this was the first snow I had seen, and me a born and bred New Englander.

Back in the next car but one I found Captain Louis Kingston, my good friend and boss who hailed from Barre, Vermont. Sure enough, and as I had expected, he was standing on the platform, drawing on his ever-present pipe and watching the snow-covered mountain range with a faraway look in his eyes.

"What does that make you think of, sir?" I asked gaily.

He turned to me and grinned his slow, friendly grin, and answered quietly,

"Your home and mine! I wonder what it's like up in the Green Mountains just now. Wouldn't you give something to go to a real sugaring-off party?"

"I certainly would," I replied, wondering how many of my Southern friends would know what a sugaring-off party really was.

Just then one of the doctors whose home was in North Carolina came along.

"What are you two Yankees up to?" he asked. "Admiring the snow on those mountains. I'll bet."

We laughingly admitted we were doing just that and then asked him if he knew about sugaring-off parties — only to have him reply, as we had expected, that he didn't.

Captain Kingston explained:

"When the sap has been collected from all the maples, there's still snow left on the ground in many places. The sap is boiled down for the syrup and sugar that you know as maple syrup and candy. It's during this process that the people who are working at the job like to pour a bit of the hot syrup slowly over good clean snow. The hardening process is so rapid that a sort of taffy forms, and let me tell you it's delicious!"

The Southern gentleman shook his head in wonderment and went away, I'm sure, with the firm conviction that Yankees were funny people.

Time passed more and more slowly, and as we neared our destination we were cautioned to be on the alert for German or Italian planes. A couple of troop trains like our own, it seems, had been bombed in that section within the past fortnight. To make matters worse, the moon was full and bright as a dollar at night, lighting up the train for miles around. The only thing we could do was to keep our fingers crossed and pray like blazes.

We learned one morning that it was to be our last day out and that we were going to be bivouacked in Constantine for a while. We were glad to be nearing the end of our journey, because it had been a long one and everyone was tired and tense. I don't think anyone had relaxed since knowing we were potential targets for Axis bombs. We finally arrived in Constantine at about 6:00 p.m. on the fifth day of our trip. All that time to cover ground that one of our crack American trains could have traversed in thirteen or fourteen hours.

The Colonel came into the car to tell us to be ready in a matter of an hour or so.

"You will all file out onto the station platform," he said, "at either side of the car. Officers on one side and nurses on the other. Follow along in formation to the English lorries that will be at the loading ramp. From here on in we are to be part of an English-conducted convoy. Remember these people are our friends and allies, and co-operate with them to the last degree."

Just then the train pulled into the station, and we could hear the voices of our limey friends as their sergeants were shouting instructions to their drivers. The clipped English accent was rather pleasant to hear after weeks of trying to understand Arabs, and the sight of the troops, with their overseas caps hanging so jauntily over the left ear, was welcome, too. We climbed eagerly into the trucks only to find that instead of having seats along the sides, as our army trucks did, this particular type of English vehicle had only a floor. I hoped we were not to be carried in the thing for long, because the pavements there were cobblestones, and each time the wheels turned we were jiggled like jelly. Those boys drove us as we had never ridden before. And even the lunge to an abrupt stop — which nearly shook our heads off our shoulders — was gratefully acknowledged to be the most gentle moment of the journey.

"All right, lydies! Everybody out, now. This is where you are to stay."

We scrambled down to the ground and had a look around. All that could be seen was a huge patch of weeds — nothing else. We could hear men's voices, but in spite of the bright moonlight nothing else was discernible.

"This can't be the place," said one of the girls in dismay. "There's simply nothing here."

"That is the general idea, little lydy," put in the English driver. "There are two 'ospital units in there under camouflage, and of course you know that you are up in the part of the country now where you wouldn't dare strike a bloody match or flash a bloody light for anything in the world. Jerry is always lurking about, and 'e gets 'is stroke of dirty work in before one knows it. Just as 'e did in London before this bloody campaign started."

Soon our Colonel and Chief came along, satisfied themselves that we were all there, and then told us to follow along behind them to the area where we were to set up our tents temporarily. This, they explained, was to be just a bivouac area, as we were to push up farther toward the front.

We started off slowly behind them, stumbling over the roots of trees and falling into depressions in the ground until finally our eyes became accustomed to the intense darkness, and then we didn't fall around quite so much. We were carrying our field equipment and were exhausted from the train trip, so our dispositions were none too sweet for the occasion. After what seemed to be an unending climb, we were finally told to sit down on the ground until a tent could be put up for us to get under. The night was intensely cold and clear, and the ground like ice. Everybody dropped down, regardless, and in a very few minutes many of the group were asleep with their heads on their musette bags.

"Are you cold, Ruthie?" asked Louise.

"I'm frozen to death," I answered through my chattering teeth.

"Maybe this will help," she said as she passed me, of all things, a bottle of Scotch.

I took it quickly and swallowed a couple of draughts and felt it burn all the way down.

"Where in heaven's name did you get this?" I asked, incredibly grateful.

"One of my friends from the Air Corps gave it to me just before we got on the train. I thought there would probably come a time when we would need it. And this sure is the time!"

She passed the precious bottle to a couple of our friends, then tucked it away for future reference. I'm sure if it had not been for that drink, and its agreeable effects, I would have perished. The colder I became, the more my back ached. Soon the enlisted men had a ward tent up for us and canvas cots put in. Our bedding rolls hadn't come in on the same train with us, so we tried as best we could to wrap up in our coats, raincoats, and such, and to get as comfortable as possible under the circumstances. I had been brought up in a cold climate all my life, but I have never suffered from the cold as I did in the few hours that passed before the welcome voice of Captain Sutton was heard exclaiming outside the tents,

"Your bedding rolls are here. Come and get them."

We hurried to the tent flap and held it back while each girl claimed her roll and one of the enlisted men carried it in and placed it on her cot for her. I unstrapped mine and climbed in with everything I had on, even to my shoes. I had always disliked my roll, but believe me, it was welcome that night. I vowed I'd never fuss again about packing and rolling the thing as gradually I began to become warm and relaxed from the warmth of the blankets. Then, at last, the relief of blessed sleep!

We were allowed to sleep in the morning as long as we cared to, because the Chief realized how little rest we had had — including herself — aboard the train. At noon it was a happier group of girls who hit the chow line and ate like little pigs.

We could see, now, that we were sitting on top of a high hill at the edge of what appeared to be a very large city. From where we were, the city seemed a modern one, and the buildings much like those in any large community at home. We immediately became curious about the place and began to ask if it would be possible to go to town. Our Colonel and Chief Nurse assured us it would not, and that our place was on the top of the hill, so it was a disappointed group of girls who made their way slowly back to the tent for another night. On the way we passed nurses from one of the other groups, dressed in blue uniforms and looking pert as fashion plates. They rather put us, in our coveralls and field jackets, to shame. I recognized one of them as a girl I had met at a party in Oran.

"Where are you girls going?" I called to her.

"Down to look the town over. Aren't you girls going to do the same?" she returned.

"Our CO. told us the town was off limits to us," said Kirk. "Maybe they don't like us around here."

Sadly we watched the girls pass on down toward the edge of the clearing, then we stood and griped for a bit It seemed reasonable that if they could go, we should be allowed to go, too, so back we started toward the headquarters tent.

As we stood around waiting for more light from the CO., who seemed to be busy at the moment, our Chief came striding out.

"What is it, girls?" she asked, sweetly. "Can I be of any help to you? The Colonel is pretty busy just now."

"Yes, Lieutenant Salter," I said, for I found myself closest to her, accidentally. "We just want to know why the city is off limits to us and not to the groups bivouacked below us. I was just talking to Jane Purdy of that group, who is a friend of mine, and the nurses and officers in that group all have permission to go down into the city. If it isn't definitely off limits, we want to go, too!"

She went into the tent and we saw her talking with the Colonel, and soon she came out with a smile on her face and said,

"The Colonel says you can go but that there must be an officer along. None of the girls are to go by themselves. The people here are Moslems, and they do not approve of women traveling around alone as we do at home. We must not do anything to offend them while we are here."

We went happily off toward the tent to get ourselves ready to go sight-seeing. On the way past the area where the officers were staying we asked one of them to walk to town with us, explaining that the Colonel had wisely changed his mind about letting us go.

Leading off the hill where we were bivouacked was a flight of stone steps that one had to go down to get into the city proper. We counted them and found there were one hundred and sixty-eight in all. Laughingly I said, "I hope there won't be that many when we start counting them the other way!"

We found, as we progressed nearer to the heart of the city, that it was laid out on different levels and each level was reached by a series of steps like those leading away from our bivouac area. There was no such a thing as a hill to be walked up in the entire town, and the automobile traffic was routed around the outside. The natives were of a different class of Arab than those we had come in contact with around Arzeu. These people were much cleaner and more intelligent-looking, although it still was a common thing to see them, male and female alike, answering nature's call at the side of the road! They appeared to be a very devout people, as all day long there was the ringing of church bells, and one would see the native men and women standing with their heads bowed and their lips moving in silent prayer.

"You know, I sometimes wish we were able to get as much comfort from our prayers as these people do," remarked one of the girls.

"I guess we are just plain heathens," I replied. "We only pray if we want something, or are scared!"

The buildings in the city were of fine, modern architecture and remarkably clean. The Europeans we met on the street seemed to be of a patrician type and not the uncouth type of a great many of the French people we came in contact with in the coastal towns. The streets were well cared for, and the parks were many and beautiful. There was the usual number of shops selling leather goods and junk jewelry to the American military, and taking them over the traces for them, too. The leather goods were beautiful, but all had the unmistakable odor of uncured hide. I discovered later there were so many American soldiers buying these goods to send home that they couldn't take time to cure the leather. Hence the odor.

"Ask someone what the building is that stands so high on the top of the hill?" said Louise.

We stopped the next man we met who looked as though he might understand what we were talking about.

"What is that building up there, sir?" asked Lieutenant Macintosh, indicating the building in question.

"That is the hospital for civilians," answered the man in perfect English. "It is run by the British. Before so many of your hospitals arrived up here, the Americans were taken there, too. But it is not nearly large enough for our present needs."

"Is this your home?" I asked.

"Yes, ma'am. I had a good business here before the war, and I hope to once again. We are glad the Americans have come to drive out our oppressors. I learned to speak English in America. I went to college there. We certainly hope you enjoy your stay in Constantine, and you must not leave without seeing the natural gorge at the outside of the business district. The town is built around it, and there is a suspension bridge over it. Perhaps the ladies might not like it, as it swings when walking on it, but it is perfectly safe, I assure you!" He tipped his hat in a very gentlemanly manner and left us.

"Well, imagine that!" exclaimed Louise. "He might be any American you would meet on Broadway and Forty-second Street."

We found our way to the gorge, and it was truly a beautiful sight: a natural gorge right in the heart of the city, and with many caves and caverns in it. The boys walked out onto the bridge, but I must confess the girls stayed behind. I wasn't used to having a bridge that moved when I did, and I wasn't crazy about trying it.

As we wandered back, not entirely sure of ourselves and where we wanted to go, we stumbled onto the native section of the city. It was called the Madena and was inhabited entirely by Arabs. There were tiny shops all along the sidewalk with native wares, and the people seemed to crowd out around you so that you couldn't go along the street to the next shop, and it was almost necessary to buy some little thing before they would separate and allow you to go on your way. As we moved along, making slow progress, an English soldier on a motorcycle drove up. At sight of him the natives disappeared as though someone had waved a magic wand.

"Are you having trouble, sir?" he asked addressing his remarks to Lieutenant Macintosh. "Perhaps you had better turn back at the next street.

These people think all soldiers have money, and they are not entirely trustworthy. Besides, sir, you wouldn't want anything to happen to the young ladies!"

"Thank you, soldier, we are glad you happened along, I was just beginning to wonder how one got out of this mess, anyhow," replied Lieutenant Macintosh.

The soldier rode slowly along beside us until we were headed back into the European section, and then, saluting smartly, he proceeded on his way. Somehow the military police in any country seem to have the situation well in hand, whether they are ours or the other fellow's. By the time we got back to our bivouac area we were the sole possessor of some dozen picture postcards and some blisters on our heels. It had been well worth it, in that it was going to be something to remember when we were old and gray. When we hit the chow line that night, we more than did justice to the food that was prepared for us. I seemed to be having trouble getting my breath and was conscious of a sense of fatigue. I made a remark about it while standing in line, and one of the doctors told me it was because we were getting so high above sea level. As we were all sitting around on the grass talking after the supper meal and discussing our various experiences as far as the city was concerned, there came to our ears the sound of the shuffling of many feet and the sound of someone talking in a foreign tongue. It didn't sound exactly like any of the languages we had been listening to, either. As the sound seemed to come from the steps at the edge of the clearing, some of the more curious of us moved over there and looked down over the edge.

"Goodness, what are those bedraggled-looking people?" asked Edna Atkins.

Just then the Colonel came along. He watched for a minute and then explained:

"Those are Italian and German prisoners. I imagine they are being taken to the French garrison, a couple of miles away. They certainly will have to stop when they reach the top of these steps, at the rate those French guards are hurrying them along."

As they progressed up the steps, they became conscious that we were watching them, and thereafter it was easy to tell which were which. The Italians grinned and threw us kisses, but the Germans just looked stolidly at us, with no change of expression, and then turned indifferently away. Sure enough, just as the Colonel said, they were halted at the top of the steps. One of our enlisted men, who could speak Italian, went over to the group and started to talk. The French guards looked displeased but didn't try to stop him. He talked pleasantly with them for a few minutes and then burst out laughing. The boys to whom he was talking seemed to think it funny, too, as they grinned at his laughter. Soon they received the order to move on, and he came back to where we were standing with the Colonel.

"What was so funny, Corporal?" asked the Colonel.

"Those Italian boys are glad to be prisoners, sir," he explained. "They say they are tired of fighting and going hungry and being left behind to cover for the Germans when things get going tough." He grinned for a second and then added, "That fellow I gave the cigarette to came from Brooklyn. He was visiting some relatives in the old country and was mustered into the army and not allowed to return to the States. When he asked me for a Lucky, in English, I nearly fainted. All in all, I guess the Italians are not crazy about this war."

We went back to our places, realizing for the first time how men looked who had been in this war game a long time. They were dirty and emaciated, and their clothes were worn, and it was obvious they had lost considerable weight. Suddenly a figure appeared at the edge of the group that looked familiar.

"Is Ginny Ayers around?" he asked.

"Jimmie!" about a dozen voices shouted. "How did you get here and when? Are the rest of the boys with you? Tell us about everything!"

Jimmie was Ginny's boy friend; he had been stationed near Arzeu with us and had been there when we left by train. Now, to see him appear right out of nowhere, was really something. The look on Ginny's face as she went toward him was something to behold, too. Two nice youngsters with an honest affection for each other, and it did your heart good to see them together!

"Just a second," he said. "One at a time, and I'll be glad to answer your questions. Yes, some of the boys are with me and will see you in due time. And the others who were left behind were all O.K. a couple of days ago. I got here by jeep going sixty miles up and down to every twenty straight ahead." As he said this, he rubbed his buttocks and winced a little as though he might be bruised a trifle.

He visited with us a while and left with the promise to come again soon.

When we were inside the tent, the Chief said:

"Get your things together tonight, for we are pulling out of here early tomorrow morning, and as I've said before, let's not have the nurses the ones to hold up the parade. We are moving by lorry and in an English convoy. I don't know where we are going, but it will be nearer the actual front. I understand we'll be about fourteen hours on the road and that there'll be rest periods every two hours for ten minutes, with a half-hour in the middle of the day for limch. Yes, C rations once again, bless them! And don't look so stricken. Miss Ayers. At least you saw your Jimmie once again, which is more than the other girls did." (And that was no joke!) "Rest well, and be on time. Good night, now."

So we were on our way again, destination unknown.

CHAPTER TEN: To Tebessa in Truck Convoy

Here we were starting out on another truck ride. This time I found myself riding with many of my old tentmates, including Glenna Whitt, Genevieve Kruszic, and Margaret Hornback. Kirk and Edna, as well as Mary Meyer and Helen Molony, were also in my lorry, so I was among friends, at least! Louise was riding up in the cab with the driver because of the crowded situation in the rear.

The English officer in charge of the convoy moved along from one vehicle to another giving us last-minute instructions.

"Fellow officers and nurses, you are going up into a zone that is very dangerous. You must constantly be on the watch for enemy planes, and it is as much your duty as that of the patrols to give notice of the approach of such planes. In case a plane is sighted, the first lorry will stop and the driver will signal with his hand to the lorry behind, and so on down the entire convoy. Everyone will leave the lorries and go over the side of the road and get quickly down to the ground. No doubt you have had instructions as to what to do in an air raid long before now. Lunch will be at noon sharp, and then you will not eat again until you reach your destination. Goodbye now, and may God be with you."

One by one the lorries in the huge convoy moved out onto the highway. The day was a beautiful one, and it had been so peaceful during our stay in bivouac that it seemed hard to realize that danger lurked now in every spot. There were three complete hospital groups moving out in the convoy, but not all of us were for the same destination. We were fairly near the front of the convoy, and as we looked back, it seemed like a huge caterpillar crawling along the road. Ships, trucks, trains! For months now we had been moving in groups for protection. It certainly would seem strange to start out all by one's self again.

As we rode along, we began to pass small talk around among ourselves, believing this the best way to keep from thinking.

I studied the faces of the various girls and thought how much they had changed in the past few months. Some of the little devil-may-care youngsters, it is true, had stood up well under difficulties, and all of them had been good soldiers. And it was also true that you could put a girl into pants and give the same treatment as a soldier, but somehow she always remained feminine. Curls popped out from under helmets, lips shone with lipstick of various hues, and all of us wore perfume or cologne of some sort.

"They can stop anytime now as far as I am concerned," volunteered Doris Friedlund.

This brought forth knowing smiles, for she was always the first of the group to want to rest and change her position.

"It won't be long before we get a ten-minute stop," consoled the Chief.

The next few minutes passed quickly, and then the lorry ahead began to slow down for a stop; and trucks with the boys dropped behind, and soon our vehicle rolled to a stop also. Then a problem presented itself. These rest periods, so called, were all well and good for the men, but we couldn't see for the life of us how thirty women clad in coveralls could answer nature's call while standing out on an open plain in almost plain view of hundreds of men. Finally the problem was solved by having four of the girls hold four blankets by the corners, thus forming an enclosure for the others, two at a time. This took care of one angle of the situation, but I still maintain the Army should fashion the G.I. gals' coveralls with drop seats!

We were soon on our way again climbing steadily. I found myself acquiring a headache that was to endure for some time, until I got adjusted to the atmospheric changes. The country all around us was beautiful; and I thought, as I had many times before, that I would like very much, someday after the war, to visit all the parts of Africa we had traversed. Farther along, there was evidence of recent bombings: huge craters in the ground and bits of airplane wreckage strewn along the road. Soon we passed an airfield on which there were seven of the planes that had never been able to get off the ground: burned to bits right on the runways. Men from the ordnance were at work on them salvaging the usable parts to repair others that weren't so badly damaged. These boys from the ordnance are the unsung heroes of the combat zones: they keep our equipment in order and many, many times make something out of practically nothing!

"Isn't that horrid?" said Glenna. "Think of the money and the labor that went into those planes, and then they didn't have a chance."

"It only goes to show what a score we have to settle over here," said Miss Hornback grimly.

"What are those things sticking out of the ground over there?" asked Mary.

As we came nearer to the objects of her curiosity, we could see they were guns, well dug in down below the ground level, their crews in the same holes with their weapons. As the convoy passed and it suddenly dawned on the crews that we were girls, they went mad. They started jumping up and down, waving their hands at us and shouting. The boys, thought I, who are at these faraway outposts, always on guard, living alone for weeks on end, are not the ones of whom headlines are made, but they are in there fighting as much as though they were the heroes. All along the way for the next few miles we passed through a solid avenue of guns. The road we were on was the direct supply line to the troops and had to be kept open at all cost. There was only one railroad running from Constantine up into this country, and we noticed, whenever we had occasion to cross it, that many attempts had been made to knock it out with bombings. Here and there were crews of our engineers at work replacing tracks that some stray bomb had knocked sky high.

Noon at last, and we stopped and pulled to the side of the road. It was time to eat our rations. Some of us had managed to wheedle a can or two of chicken out of the kitchen crew, and I had a can of luncheon meat of which I was very proud. So Louise and I and Glenna didn't do too badly. I found that my mouth and gums were becoming very sore from the lack of fruit and fresh vegetables, and at that point I don't know what I would have given for a glass of milk or a head of lettuce! All along the way we passed Arabs, with their herds of sheep and goats. It seemed strange to see them grazing right in the middle of an area where our soldiers would have anywhere from one to a half dozen of our "big babies" dug in with their noses pointed skyward. They didn't pay any attention to the guns, and the gun crews seemed to ignore them. More and more the signs of war were becoming evident. Luck must have been with us, because we hadn't had any trouble up to then.

"Why are the men removing the cover from the gun?" asked Kruszic, pointing to the cab of the lorry behind us. Farther behind, the men in the other lorries were doing likewise.

"At this time of day they are more than ever on the alert for raiders," answered Lieutenant Salter. "Sundown and sunrise are the times when they're most likely to attack, for it's difficult to see them if they fly straight out of the sun. Before you realize it, they are overhead."

This startling bit of information made us even more tense, and I think we were all very happy when the sun at last disappeared.

"Remember, girls, no cigarettes after sunset. The flare of a match can be seen for an awfully long way," cautioned the Chief.

As it grew dark, it became colder, and the wind that had started to blow ever so slightly now had teeth in it. It seemed that even with all the clothes we could get on, it was still biting cold in that part of the country. I was beginning to wonder how much farther we might have to go when we came into view of a city that seemed to be entirely encircled by a wall. As we drew up to it, the convoy stopped, and the officer in the front vehicle got out and went into what appeared to be a headquarters of some kind. Soon he came out, gave the signal for us to proceed, and took the convoy out around the walled area instead of through it. We were curious to know what it was all about.

"This must be Tebessa. There is a sign that says so!" exclaimed one of the girls.

"Yes, I think that it is," agreed the Chief. "We've still about twelve miles to go."

"What sort of place is it?" I asked.

"I don't really know. But it has some sort of religious significance, and it's off limits to military personnel unless on official business."

I smiled to myself in the semidarkness at the thought of how readily Lieutenant Salter could find these bits of information to give us, yet when we asked her a direct question about things that didn't actually concern us, we always got a polite "I don't know" for an answer. We shifted our positions and tried to get a little more comfortable for the last stretch of our trip. Every once in a while I could hear a rumble in the distance that sounded like thunder, but which my good common sense told me was the rumble of heavy artillery.

"Sounds like business up there," said Helen Molony.

"Well, it doesn't sound as if they were making love," retorted Mary.

"I wonder how far away it is?" asked Kruszic. "It doesn't sound so near as when we came ashore, and then it was several miles away."

"Whose courage are you bolstering? Mine or yours?" I said jokingly.

Soon we appeared to be climbing straight up a mountainside, and such a bumping and banging around I had never before experienced. I wondered what might be the answer to the situation, when all of a sudden we could hear Major Proffitt's voice. He was the adjutant and had been in the advance party sent up to break camp for us. At least that meant that we had arrived, and none too soon. Finally the lorry stopped and we began to jump down.

"Are you girls hungry?" asked Major Proffitt.

"We'll eat anything cheerfully, sir," answered one of the girls. She wasn't kidding, either.

Under a bright moon we succeeded in locating the mess tent on the side of an adjoining hill, about three quarters of a mile away. We were set up in camouflage again and well dispersed. The rumble of gunfire was more pronounced now, and we could hear the rumble of tanks going on up to the front.

"Above all, do not flash a light," snapped the officer of the guard. "I have orders to shoot first and ask questions after, if a light is shown in camp. We are sitting in Jerry's lap, here, and anything may happen. Be good soldiers and don't take chances."

We stumbled and fell over each other on the way to the mess tent, but when we arrived, we certainly didn't take long to get into line and then to sink down on the ground to eat the hot meal that our cooks had prepared for us. Coffee without sugar and cream, but hot, and warming to our chilled bodies. Then we were directed back down from the mess and started to our quarters. By now it was well after nine o'clock and I don't think that, even though we were where we were, anyone would have had to be rocked asleep. We were all exhausted. By the time we reached the tent we were to live in, the enlisted men had our bedding rolls in and were bringing the cots. Many of us hung around outside and helped to set up the cots before they were carried in, because at least we had the light of the moon outside, which was more than we had in the tent. Finally we got them in and found we must dig in for the legs on the high side, for we were on a hill at almost a forty-five-degree angle. Even so I hung on, all that first night, to keep from rolling out of bed. We certainly presented a peculiar sight when daylight arrived and we could see the way we had been sleeping; but strangely enough, nobody gave much of a darn.

"Where is the latrine?" asked one of the girls and then grinned a little because last night we had taken refuge behind any old tree. But daylight was a different matter!

"Down the hill and to the right and keep going. Whoever laid out this camp surely was heaven-bent on getting our tents well dispersed," replied the Chief.

When the girl in question returned, she was puffing and panting as though she never would make it.

"Goodness," she gasped. "I'll bet it's a good quarter of a mile straight down this hill to the latrine. It most certainly would never do to be in a hurry!"

"Let's go to mess, Haskell," said Louise. "By the time we get over to that area it will be time to eat, I know. Pass me my mess kit, will you? There on the ground behind you."

I picked up her mess kit and my own, and we started slowly along for the cook tent, which from that point we were unable to see.

"I wonder what they did with the water tank," I said, for my canteen needed filling.

I had no sooner finished speaking than we stepped out around what appeared to be a clump of bushes but on closer inspection proved to be the tank in question. It was camouflaged so well it wasn't even recognizable from a few feet away. We filled our canteens and then kept on toward the sound of voices on the next hill. Again we couldn't make out the cook tent from the trees and foliage, but we could hear the voices of Sergeant Roberts and his boys, and to us that spelled food.

It was comparatively quiet, but now and then a round of artillery fire could be heard and the occasional drone of a plane as it passed quickly overhead. I know that I for one was always glad when the sound of the motor, and its even hum, identified it as our own. It seemed that the German planes were not carburetor-fed, and so the sound of their motors could be recognized. Even the girls quickly learned to know when Jerry was overhead and when it was one of ours.

About the time we reached the area of the mess, the boys started to serve and the line moved quickly. We just dropped down on the ground anyplace as soon we had received our rations. As we sat there, all in one group, a sudden whir was heard and two planes swooped down off the mountaintop directly back of us, so near we could almost reach up and touch them. It startled us pretty much, and the guards identified them as Italian, evidently of the reconnaissance type since they did not trouble us. Our C.O.'s face looked troubled as he watched them out of sight. It sometimes worried him a great deal to have the responsibility of us girls on his hands in that particular zone of operations. After we had finished eating, he stepped forward and addressed us:

"Members of this command: as you have seen, we are set up here in camouflage, which is not the usual procedure for a hospital group. If we were set up and functioning as a hospital, we would be out in the open and use the Red Cross marking on the ground. But as we are only bivouacked, we have to be careful about giving away the location of our camp site. I am glad those two planes passed over just when they did, for it brings home the points I want to bring out to you at this time. You are now sitting together in a single group. Your mess kits are lying open, reflecting the sunlight. This is something that you must watch out for. When you stand in the chow line, hold your mess kits, which are aluminum, away from the sun, in the shadow of your body. And when you have received your rations, move off into the shadow of the trees to eat, not out here in the open. Another thing: when those planes passed over, you instinctively looked up. You must learn not to do this. That is the reason why the soldier in combat smears dirt on his face, so there will be no reflection of light from it as he watches the sky. Another thing, practice dispersion among yourselves. Do not gather in large groups. If one of those planes had dropped an egg just now, he would have wiped out this entire outfit.

"We shall only be here for a few days, for we are to separate into two groups again, as we did back at the coast. The first unit will move to the north and the second unit to the east. There will probably be forty miles or so between us, and in this way we can take care of patients from a wider area of the front. The operating team will work with the second unit for the time being and will go where needed the most as time goes on. Try to exercise care while we are here in this area, for our very safety and the finishing of the job we came over here to do depends on it."

He strode off down the hill, and gradually everybody else started down the hill toward their quarters. We had certainly had an object lesson brought home to us, and it was giving us something to think about. As we reached the bottom of the hill, crossed the gully, and started up the next one to go to the tent that was our quarters, we could hear the rumble of the treads of the tanks still moving on up. When we came to a break in the trees, we could see them on the road down below us, tank after tank, with a man and a gun in the turret. We watched for a few minutes and then continued on our way. As we reached the tent, we found the girls crowded around Lieutenant Salter, who was explaining about a cross we would have to make out of sheets and place on the ground for identification purposes.

"This," said she, "is known as the Geneva Cross and is the sign agreed upon at the Geneva Conference after the last war to be used to mark a hospital site. The Germans, so far, have really observed this and have not deliberately fired upon any hospital."

It was to be a rather large affair, ninety by ninety feet, so that we were in for a great deal of sewing. Everyone stayed in the tent after chow, and we worked in groups of two. Each girl started sewing at opposite ends of two sheets and met in the middle. When we had enough sewed together, we started the second group, to serve as the intersecting arm of the cross. It was a beautiful day outside, and some of us did not like to sew; but this was to be our protection, and I felt we should all work on it so that it would be finished by the time we were ready to move out and set up as a hospital proper.

As we worked along diligently inside the tent, the voice of the guard above us on top of the hill barked out fiercely,

"Who in blazes does that laundry belong to? Hey, youse down there. Take those things off the tent ropes. What are youse trying to do, leave a calling card so they can find us without trouble? Women, women, more trouble than they're worth!"

The girl whose towels were hanging on the tent rope outside turned a delicate shade of scarlet and hurried out to remove them. Lesson number two learned the hard way: first the incident of the planes, and then this.

Time passes quickly when one sews. There were sheets to the left of us and sheets to the right of us, and personally I couldn't see anything that even faintly resembled a cross about the whole thing, but I guess it must have been all right. For two long afternoons we sewed on sheets until the sun went down, and then there wasn't much left to do but go to bed, as we couldn't have any light. There were the usual song fests and gab fests, and occasional tears here and there from some girl lonesome for her honey, and the usual amount of griping about the food, the camp area, and the Army in general. We were rapidly becoming field soldiers with a vengeance.

The next morning, when it came time to get up and go to the mess, Lieutenant Salter told us we had better get ready to get our bedding rolls in order once again, as Unit One would move out sometime within the next two days and it would be much simpler for us if we were nearly ready to go at any time. So after chow we came back to the tent and started packing our rolls again. As I worked, bent over in a stooped position, my back really began to give me trouble, and as I started to straighten up I found myself unable to do so. Louise noticed I was having trouble and came over and started talking in an undertone:

"You are just a plain dope if you don't tell somebody about that back. So help me, if you don't pretty soon, I will. You can't go on like this."

"You are a fussbudget," I grimaced at her. "I'm all right for a long time yet. I'll turn in when I can't stand it any longer. We've a job to do, gal, and I'm thinking that before we get through here, every pair of hands will be needed. Let's not worry about me any more, what say?"

We finished with the rolls, and then she and I went down to join one of our officer friends at the bottom of the hill. She told him I was in pain, and he gave me some medicine that took care of the situation for me. Bless my good friends! (And I was to find I had many of them.)

The next day we were told we were to move out the following morning and were given instructions as to how we would set up in the field and what each girl's post would be. I dreaded another truck ride, but such was life at that point.

The next day, promptly at nine, the equipment personnel and all of Unit One were in trucks ready to start. Many of the girls in the second unit were crowded around the tailboard of the trucks talking to us, and we had a mighty queer feeling in our hearts, for this was the first time the outfit as a whole had been divided since we came overseas. Many friends were being separated for the first time since they had come into the Army. As the trucks rolled away and we waved at the gang remaining behind until we passed out of sight, a great many of the girls' eyes were pretty bright and they were blinking rapidly as they tried not to let the tears fall. Unit Two was to make their move within a day or so, but it was remaining in the bivouac area for the time being.

The truck convoy was smaller this time than any we had moved in before. Major Frederick Mackenbrock was in charge and was the commanding officer of the unit, now that we were operating as a separate hospital. He was a quiet, shy sort of person but well liked by the personnel. As we rolled along through the countryside the natives looked at us without much expression on their faces. I guess so much had happened to them and to their country in the past few months that nothing surprised them any more. They took only a passing look at the trucks and then continued about their business. Here and there a truck load of English soldiers would pass us and shout and wave in greeting. We went back through Tebessa — that is, through the part of the city that was outside the wall — and beyond. Then we branched off onto a different road than that which we had followed into the city. The road wound round and round the mountains, and the trucks careened around the curves in a frightening manner. They really weren't driving very fast, but being able to see the sheer drop down from the roadbed made it rather exciting. I have never known a G.I. soldier to drive in convoy other than in a sensibly safe manner, but sometimes the territory itself scares one to death. Soon the truck began to slow down, then turned off the road entirely and plunged upon a plateau of sorts. After that, we heard the voices of the forward echelon call in greeting,

"So you got here at last? What held you up? We expected you quite some time ago. When did you start? Are you hungry?"

It seemed we were always arriving somewhere, hungry! But then the old faithful kitchen crew usually had our chow ready for us in a hurry if it wasn't already waiting for us when we arrived. We scrambled down and looked over the sight of our new home. Whereas the last camp had been on a mountainside, and in the trees, this one was on a plateau that stretched for miles all around us, and not a tree in sight. A short distance away from where the trucks had stopped was a huge plot of tall cactus plants. The kind that didn't have prickles, thank goodness, because some G.I. on the latrine detail had conceived the bright idea of placing the girls' latrine tent smack dab in the middle of the cactus patch! I'll bet there was many a smile on the enlisted men's faces when they saw one of us strolling nonchalantly up toward the cactus patch!

After chow at noon. Lieutenant Salter called us together and told us that instead of the large tent we had lived in at Arzeu, wall tents accommodating two people had been set up for us, and for the most part we would live two girls to a tent, although there would be one pyramidal tent with five of the girls in it.

"Lieutenant Haskell, you and Lieutenant Miller will live together in that tent at the top of the rise over there. It is at the outside edge of the area, but the guard passes almost directly behind the tent as he makes his rounds during the night. You won't be frightened, will you?" she asked.

We assured her we wouldn't, which was a lie; then we picked up our equipment and started for what was to be our home for a while. We were both rather pleased over the prospect of living together, as I had become very fond of my little Rebel friend; and although we were two entirely different types, we got along unusually well together. As we walked along,

Mary and Helen ran by us, and we found they were to be our neighbors. Soon all the girls had been assigned to quarters, and we went about the business of setting up light housekeeping.

"Louise," I suggested, "what say we go down and inspect the hospital setup when we've finished here?" I had talked with one of the boys before chow, and he had said that the receiving office, headquarters, the X-Ray tent, and the operating-room tent were all set up, as well as several of the wards. I had also learned I was to work for Captain Kingston and Captain Giest again, and I wanted to see my ward and see if it was equipped at all. First come, first served, was the rule in this game of supplies.

"O.K.," she agreed. "I'll be right with you as soon as I find my comb. My hair doesn't look as though it had been combed for a month, and I can't wear this little old knit cap forever."

I waited until she combed her hair, then we started down the hill. Several of the girls in the other tents called out to us and asked where we were living, and invited us in for a cigarette, so somehow or other it was late afternoon and we hadn't been down into the hospital area. Frequently there were ominous sounds to the north of us, but we hadn't seen a plane in two days. We had found out that the nurses' tents had been set up on one side of the road and the officers' tents on the opposite side, with the enlisted personnel in their shelter halves, or pup tents as they called them, just to the left of the officers' area. From this area down to the main road was the hospital site. Soon it was chow time, and we hit the old line again for food. We were still eating outside, as there hadn't been time for a tent to be set up to get us under cover. As we were standing around eating, I was rather amused to overhear two enlisted men talking together. One of them was saying,

"Hardtack! I'm God-damned tired of it! We live a dog's life all right — wear dog tags, eat dog biscuits, and sleep in pup tents!"

The boy really had something there. These kids would gripe about little things, but you surely could depend on them in a pinch.

It soon started to get dark, and very rapidly. It seemed strange to me, but there was not any twilight, nor for that matter any dawn in this country. The sun just seemed to sink rapidly out of sight in the late afternoon, and then it was pitch black and night had fallen. It was just the opposite in the morning. When we got up for duty at six-thirty it would be night outside, and as we went to work at seven the sun would be in the heavens, shining brightly.

That seemed to settle the fact that we would have to inspect the hospital the next day. I wondered when we would get our first patients.

CHAPTER ELEVEN: Life in a Field Hospital

The Corporal of the Guard woke me in what seemed like the middle of the night to announce that a few patients had been brought back from the front and were being treated at Tent 1A. Would I please report there as quickly as possible?

"I'll be right there," I said, "but what time is it, anyhow?" It was so dark I could barely see his face.

"Six o'clock. Do you know where 1A is?"

It dawned on me suddenly that we hadn't been able to get down into the hospital area the day before and that I didn't really know where my ward tent was. When I confessed the truth, he said he would wait at the guard post and take me there when I was ready.

I scrambled out of bed, trying to be quiet so as not to awaken Louise, but with the usual lack of success.

"Where are you going, Yankee?" she mumbled sleepily.

Just as I started to tell her I was going to work, the sound of metal on metal announced chow, and Sergeant Roberts' voice began shouting from somewhere outside the tent:

"Come and get it while it's hot!"

"There's nothing like breakfast in the dark," Louise groaned, sitting up in bed and fumbling for her shoes. By the time I was ready to leave the tent to join the guard, her head was buried in her suitcase and she was throwing things left and right in a frantic search for her comb. There was always something she wanted but couldn't find.

As I stepped outside, dawn was just breaking, and I believe that the sight of the sun coming up over the horizon, and the ever-changing panorama of colors around us as we — the guard and myself — walked down into the hospital area, was one of the most breathtaking moments in my life.

"Isn't that beautiful?" I cried.

"It kinda gives you the feeling of being close to God," my escort replied solemnly. "I sometimes think, when there's only the horrible around us, God tries to remind us that there's beauty still over the horizon."

I gazed at him in astonishment. There was so much about our enlisted personnel we did not know, and probably never would have time to investigate. I really was glad to have him say that the tent just ahead was the one in which I was to go to work, for I didn't know what to say to him after that last remark.

"Hello, there," said Corporal Frank Krist. "Are we going to work with you. Lieutenant Haskell?"

"I guess you are," I replied. "Who is we?"

"Calcaterra, O'Rourke, and myself. There are only a few patients now. But from what the ambulance driver said who brought these boys back, we're apt to be pretty busy at any time. Our old friends of the First Division are up ahead. This boy over here says they're happy in the knowledge that we're backing them up."

The good old First Division! The same boys we had known in England and again down at the coast. I hated the thought of anything happening to these soldiers, and if they were going to need us I was glad to be there.

I stepped over to speak to the soldier whom Corporal Krist had referred to and found a young second lieutenant, apparently in considerable pain.

"What seems to be the trouble, fella?" I asked. I noticed he kept one hand on his back.

"Forget it, nurse. Not a scratch on me. I just hurt my back getting out of a tank during a counterattack back there. The darned thing caught fire, and I guess a couple of the boys got it bad. They're over there on that side," and he nodded in the direction he wished to indicate. "How's about checking up on them and letting me know?"

"Surest thing," I said. "But first let's see what I can do to make you comfortable." I started to turn him over but he insisted vigorously that I must look after his boys first.

I crossed to the other side of the tent, and I couldn't help closing my eyes for a moment as I stepped alongside the first bed. A splendid-looking young man lay there with almost the entire surface of his face and chest burned. He had been dressed with sulfadiazine ointment, and the dressings had been left uncovered, which was the way all burns were being treated as far as possible. In the bed at the other side of him lay another young man who was also burned, but not so badly. He was fumbling with a match with his one good hand in an effort to light a cigarette. One arm was horribly distorted and burned.

"Here, soldier, let me do that," I said as I took the match from his hand.

"Hello, where did you come from?" he asked. "This isn't such a bad war, after all."

"Is there anything I can get for you?" I countered. It was a very bad war and we both knew it.

"You sure can," he said. "A hamburger and a bottle of beer would go right well at this point. How's about it?"

I looked at him wisely and we both laughed. Was it any wonder one developed a profound respect for boys like these?

I passed on about the tent, attending to the needs of other boys and observing with satisfaction that Lady Luck had smiled on me once again, inasmuch as the three corpsmen assigned to help me were real workers and had a little initiative. I had just finished washing the hands and face of one of the patients, who was suffering from a gunshot wound of the inner side of his left arm, when "Smiley" O'Rourke came up to us.

"Well," he asked, "how're we doing?"

"These are swell kids," I said.

The soldier who wanted the hamburger and beer was grimacing now with pain, but when he caught me looking, he waved with his one good hand. I returned to the young officer I had spoken to first. He appeared to be asleep; but as I turned away, he reached out his hand and caught mine. His eyes were moist as he said,

"God bless you, nurse, and the others like you. Don't think we don't realize what most of you have given up to be over here. And don't think every last one of us doesn't love you for it. My wife is a nurse in a station hospital in the States, just waiting to get into foreign duty. I couldn't see her doing it, at first. Now I'm pretty damned proud of her wanting to." He paused a moment and then asked grimly, "How are my boys?"

"They're doing O.K.," I said.

"The best damned lot of boys an officer ever had." His face clouded. "I'm afraid there aren't so many of them left after yesterday." Suddenly he broke off, wincing as if in great pain.

"Where is it?" I asked.

When he didn't reply, I turned him over and bathed his back with alcohol. As I passed my hands gently down over his sacroiliac region, I could feel him grow tense. He certainly had all my sympathy, for that was the place that I ached ninety-eight per cent of the time. Before I had finished with him. Captain Kingston came into the tent. He saw me and started down toward where I was working.

"Everything under control, I see," he began in his quiet way. "I'm glad, because I've just come from headquarters. A runner was just here from the battalion aid station, and he tells us there are about fifty others on their way to us now. Just fill the ward tents as they come in. We're going to evacuate them as soon after admission as possible." He looked down at the young lieutenant. "What seems to be the matter with this young fellow?"

"I don't know, sir, but there seems to be something wrong with his back." I explained that he was very tender and sore down through the lumbar region and could hardly stand the pressure of my hands. Then I stepped out of the way so the Captain could get in close enough to examine him.

As I watched this good friend and superior of mine, I marveled at the sensitive hands and at the way the patients reacted to his genial personality. Soon he had made his diagnosis and we had the lieutenant strapped with wide strips of adhesive. Then I gave him a sedative.

"Thanks, a lot," he whispered as we turned him again on his back. "I feel much better now. Maybe I can sleep. Captain, sir, I hope you'll take good care of my boys."

The Captain assured him he would, and we passed along from patient to patient, doing a dressing here and there and always leaving behind us a few pleasant words and a smile. As we passed on to the outside of the tent, the Captain tinned to me and said,

"How's your back?"

"What back, sir?" I retorted, feigning surprise.

He smiled, his gentle, kindly smile and shook his head. I"'ve known for some time that it was giving you trouble. It's just that your damned Yankee pride won't let you know when it's time to give up and get yourself taken care of. I want to examine you some day when we have the time."

"Yes, sir!" I said. "Some day when we have the time." And I made him promise for the present we should forget about it.

As we finished our cigarettes, the ambulances began to turn in down by the receiving office. I hurried back into the tent and told the boys to turn down the remaining beds as we had business arriving by the front gate. All too soon those beds were filled, and we were thereafter busy as bees. Dressings here, hypodermics there, a man being put up in traction for a fractured leg in one corner of the tent, and a man having his arm put into a cast in another. As the litter bearers brought us our patients, they told us the operating room was working constantly; and as I passed outside for a second to get some rocks to use as weights on the traction, I saw several corpsmen giving patients plasma as they waited on the ground for their turn on the operating table. The doctors were marvelous, the nurses were doing their job well, but I couldn't help feeling we would have been absolutely lost if it hadn't been for the unfailing loyalty and stamina of our corpsmen.

After several hours we had all the patients in bed and taken care of. Most of the girls had been on duty all day, and as it was growing dark others came now to care for the boys for the night. Doris Friedlund had joined me at noon, and we had both been so busy we hadn't had a second to speak. Glenna Whitt came to relieve us for the night, and I was glad to leave my patients in her hands. A nice girl and a good nurse. I sent Doris along off duty, and I stayed on a short while longer because in the field, as in a hospital at home, records must be kept on patients, and these had not been entered in the books because we had been so busy since their arrival. As I got ready to leave. Corporal Krist's voice came out of the dusk:

"Are you ready to go up to your tent. Lieutenant Haskell? Lieutenant Miller is waiting for us at 2B. I saw her a short time ago and told her to wait there for us. It is too dark outside for you girls to be wandering around alone with these darned Arabs nosing about. Besides, there have been a great many foxholes dug around the area today, and I don't want you girls to be falling into them and breaking your lily white necks!"

I smiled at the impudence of the young devil but hadn't the heart to say anything to him in the light of his thoughtfulness. Louise joined us at her tent, and we started across the area.

"What is that light-appearing spot over there?" Louise asked, nudging me with an elbow.

"That is the large cross you girls made while we were in bivouac up on the mountainside," replied Corporal Krist. "It is weighted down with rocks, and I imagine it can be seen for quite a distance from the air."

"Let's sincerely hope so," Louise commented.

The cross was in the middle of the area, and the hospital and living area were grouped around all sides of it. They had also put a smaller one, I later discovered, up on the hill above the living quarters.

As we reached the tent which was our home for the time being, both Louise and I thanked the young corporal for his kindness, and he strode off in the dark singing softly to himself as though he didn't have a care in the world. We were just going to step into our tent when the voice of one of our officer friends sounded out of the darkness:

"Ruth, Louise. Are you there? Are you hungry? I traded some cigarettes with an Arab for a basket of eggs. We're cooking them down in our tent, if you want to join us."

We replied we certainly did and stepped along beside him, each of us holding one of his hands. We felt our way along because I hadn't seen the area by daylight since the foxholes had been dug, and I didn't know just when to expect to fall on my face. We made the tent without any casualties, and as we stepped inside, the smell of fried eggs reached our nostrils. Once the tent flap was firmly secured from the inside, one of the boys lit a candle. I looked hurriedly around and saw a heaping mess kit full of scrambled eggs. It looked like enough for the Army, but the four of us surely made fast work of getting rid of them. After we were settled back on the cots, enjoying the cigarettes we kept cupped into our hands although we were inside, I asked:

"What has been puzzling me is how you cooked these eggs? Surely they didn't come precooked from your Arab."

"Mac, you tell them," piped up Limey. "It was your idea."

"Well, girls," said Mac, "it's like this. You see this can? It has some G.I. alcohol in it and some absorbent cotton. It makes a very good stove, although hotter than blazes. I nearly burned my hand off hanging on to my mess kit, and I guess it didn't do the blasted thing any good." He held up the kit, which was burned black on the bottom, and made a rueful face at it. Louise and I offered to clean it as our contribution to the evening.

"Now," he said, "you're talking. Now I can relax and digest those eggs."

As we walked along to our tent, Louise laughed suddenly and said,

"Ruthie, I had a very good time in there, and I think everyone else did. You know, I always used to think you had to spend a lot of money and go where there was music and good food and dancing to have fun. Africa has done much for me. My boy friend won't know me!"

Just then we reached our tent, and I must confess that when we stepped inside and busied ourselves securing the flaps before lighting a candle, our hearts were in our throats. Purely a feminine reaction, this being afraid in the dark, but it was one we never got over. I don't know really what we expected to happen, but we always sighed with relief after the tiny glow of candlelight showed us we were alone in the tent.

We hurriedly got into our bedding rolls and were talking quietly between ourselves when we heard the drone of a plane. Instantly we were up on our elbows straining our ears to listen.

"Is that a Jerry?" I asked.

"I'm not sure," Louise replied. "Let's be quiet for a minute. There seems to be more than one of them."

Rapidly the sound grew nearer, and there were evidently several planes. We weren't any too far from the front, and we had seen much evidence of the destruction wrought by bombing and strafing on our trip up here by truck. Soon it was possible to identify the motors as German. We waited expectantly until the sound began to fade away, and when it was clear they had passed over the camp area, we began to relax a little. But we had no more than settled back on our cots when they began to circle back over us again. It was one of their favorite tricks. While they wouldn't deliberately fire on a hospital, nothing prevented them from fighting a battle of nerves. And they did. At last they disappeared in the distance, and peace and quiet reigned for the night.

The next morning, just as the patients had finished chow, the ambulances rolled in to evacuate those who were able to be moved back to the nearest evacuation hospital, some forty miles to the rear. We got the patients ready as soon as possible. The gratitude of those boys, as they thanked us for all we had done for them, was payment enough for the fatigue we had endured the night they were brought in. One would think they had known us always, and it had really been less than twenty-four hours.

As the young officer was placed in the ambulance which contained his two young friends, he looked at me and said, "Thanks a million. We'll never forget you. Good luck and happy landings."

Then he was whisked away, and I knew I should never see him again.

We went about the business of straightening up the ward, and even in tents we tried to keep some semblance of hospital cleanliness. This was made very difficult because of the absence of floors, and every time the wind blew, a film of dust settled down over everything. Before we had finished, the ambulances started rolling in again and we were full to capacity once more. Some of the new boys, we discovered, were from the companies of some of our officer friends, and we were glad to have news of them and to learn they were all right. It was pathetic enough to receive some nice boy, all shot or burned to pieces, but when you found that you knew that boy it made it much more difficult to take care of him impersonally.

Days passed. Sometimes we worked fourteen and sixteen hours and were exhausted afterward, and at other times, between offensives, we sat around and wished for something to do. To make up for the busy times, we only stayed on duty half day during the lax periods, half of us working in the afternoons and half in the mornings. The night nurses were on duty only a week at a time because of the difficulty of sleeping in the daytime in the tents. Quarters were so close together that it was impossible for them to have the benefit of quiet. One particular day, just as we were admitting a group of patients, one of the boys from headquarters came running over to tell us we were to place them all back in the ambulances and send them on to the nearest evacuation hospital, as we had received orders to break camp and move. So back into the ambulances they went, after we had given them hot coffee and changed a few of the most soiled of the dressings that had been put on at the battalion aid station.

We started packing our equipment; and as we were putting everything into the wooden packing boxes that were stored from one move to another, I turned to Corporal Krist.

"Look, fella," I said, "do you suppose these could be packed and marked so that this time we could get back our own equipment when we set up again? I'm tired of getting my sterile goods and medicines just the way I want them and then, when we set up, having it to do all over again. Besides, we worked hard washing those pajamas that Smiley is packing, and I'd like to be sure we get them back again."

The Corporal thought for a minute and then said,

"Maybe I can get some luminous paint from Utilities and mark the outside of the boxes. Then if we have to set up in the dark, which is more than likely to be the case, we could readily identify them."

Matching his actions to his words, he strode off toward Utilities, and in a very few minutes the boxes containing our ward equipment were marked to his satisfaction and mine. Those corpsmen had proven jewels to work with, and I could always trust them to get things done right.

Satisfied that matters were taking care of themselves, I went off up to my tent. I wondered if Louise had gone, and I stopped at 2B, where I found her chatting with two soldiers.

"Oh, hello. I didn't see you there. Are you ready to go up to the tent?" she asked.

"I sure am," I said. "And if we don't hurry, the tent will be taken down right over our very heads. The detail seems to be starting on them now."

We arrived at our tent just in time to have the boys drag our bedding rolls out onto the ground before they pulled up the stakes and took the thing down. By the time we were packed and rolled and were closing our suitcases, the detail in charge of the baggage arrived to put them onto the trucks. Less than five hours, and what had been a busy hospital area a few minutes before was now just an open plateau. The usual group of Arabs stood around watching with much interest, and one wondered if they were really as blank as the expressions on their faces suggested. All along I had been inclined to doubt it.

After a five-hour ride in the ambulances we came into a section marked hospital area and turned off the main road and started over the worst road I have ever ridden in my life, only to arrive in a very few minutes at a group of buildings clearly identified by the huge red crosses which were stretched out on the ground beside them. We were naturally very curious and were straining our necks to see, when someone said:

"Isn't that Lieutenant Archard?"

"It is, and that is Major Proffitt over there, too!" exclaimed another girl.

As the ambulances rolled to a stop and the drivers opened the back doors for us to get down, we found we had joined our second unit temporarily, and were we glad to see our old friends once again! Nobody seemed to know why we were together, but nobody seemed to care as long as it was so. We stood around a while exchanging experiences. It happened that we had arrived just at chow time and so joined their chow line eagerly. As soon as we had finished, I set out to look up Vaughn Fisher. She took me all over their hospital, and they certainly had an ideal setup, for with real buildings they didn't have the dust to contend with.

The patients were on cots the same as ours, and the girls were wearing overseas seersucker uniforms instead of the coveralls we had grown used to. Still, I wouldn't have exchanged places with any one of them.

The evening was passed with singing and reminiscing, and then we retired to sleep in barracks for the first time in many weeks. For a while I couldn't sleep at all because of the lack of air, so I guess I had been more content living in a tent than I had thought. Finally, along toward morning, I dropped off, only to have Glenna Whitt tell me it was chow time almost before I realized I had been asleep.

We still hadn't received any orders to go to work, so we spent the day mending our clothes and welcomed the chance to wash our coveralls in the trough evidently intended for the purpose of washing clothes. One of the enlisted men was in charge of heating some water for us in a couple of G.I. cans, and we really were getting down to the business of getting our clothes clean again. Washing underthings and socks in what water one could get into a helmet, most of the time cold water at that, wasn't very conducive to clean laundry.

"I swear, Haskell," said Glenna, "these clothes of mine have tattletale gray if ever I saw any!"

"Gal," I said, "that's because you haven't been Luxing them. Don't you ever listen to the radio?"

"Oh, my bones, guess I'm getting old," said Louise as she straightened up and stretched to get the kinks out of her back and shoulders.

"You haven't seen any Arabs trying to swap electric washing machines, have you?" somebody asked cutely.

Suddenly there was a sound of excited voices and rushing feet. Before I knew what was happening, I found myself running with the others toward the compound in front of the barracks.

"Messerschmitts," somebody said from behind a large pair of field glasses, and I looked up in time to see six of them speeding along the horizon. Some distance beyond our area was an airplane ordnance field, and it was there they were obviously headed. In a few seconds fighter planes took to the air, and the dogfight was on.

We watched them duck in and out, coming up beneath each other, all the time firing with all they had. The air was filled with the staccato sound of their fire. They really weren't very far away, and we got a wonderful view. When it was evident our fighters were getting the better of things, the Messerschmitts turned as one and high-tailed it for home, this time passing directly over where we were standing. We were all thrilled to pieces to be witnessing such a sight, but then the angry voice of Major Mackenbrock broke in upon us savagely.

"Of all the darned fool performances I ever saw!" said he, crawling rapidly out of a foxhole. "Here I have all my men with their noses in the ground, and wearing helmets, and my nurses stand out in an open area, bareheaded, watching the show! Whatever were you thinking of, or weren't you thinking?" He turned to Lieutenant Salter. "I'm ashamed of you, the chief nurse, standing out here with your girls, inviting disaster. Women, women, women! Just when you think you can depend on them, bang, they go feminine on you!"

"But, sir," protested Lieutenant Salter, "this is a hospital area."

"Oh, I know. So it is. They probably wouldn't bother a hospital. But in a war we don't take fool chances." After a pause he smiled a bit and added,

"Not that I don't admire such courage and audacity. The truth of it is, I do!"

We all looked a little sheepish and went back into our barracks. Lieutenant Salter arrived a few seconds later very red in the face from a little private chat with the Major. She tried to look severe, and must have perceived the twinkle that was in everybody's eyes, because she burst out laughing, and when she did we all went off in a gale of laughter ourselves that must have been heard for miles. It seemed we would never stop, but finally we got control of ourselves, and Lieutenant Salter, wiping a tear from her eyes, said,

"Seriously, girls, the Major was right. We mustn't let it happen again. You can be buried for being too foolish out here." She grinned a bit and added, "Anyway I'm glad we had a ringside seat for one good dogfight before someone pounded a little sense into us, aren't you?"

We agreed we were immeasurably glad and thrilled to have seen it, and now we began wondering how much damage had been done to the ordnance field before the fighter planes drove them off. We had seen them drop a few eggs, and we had seen smoke rise from the ground not long after, and so anything might have happened. That night at chow a couple of the second unit girls said they had received a few patients from that area with burns and shrapnel but that the actual damage to the field had been slight. Our planes had been too fast getting into the air.

After chow that night I did not feel particularly well, and as I crossed the compound to go to my barracks to rest, the old pain started across my back, and when I reached the barracks I was crying and stumbling because of the old pain and a new one that radiated down my right leg. As I walked, I seemed to drag my right leg, and it frightened me because I had been conscious of a tired, aching sensation in that leg for several days. The barracks was empty and I quickly went to bed, hoping to get to sleep before the others came in. But instead of growing better, the pain grew steadily worse, and I was crying aloud when the girls came in and found me.

"Ruth, honey, whatever is the matter?" asked Glenna.

"It's the pain in my back," I confessed between spasms. "Please ask Lieutenant Salter to get me some codeine." I hated to be such a baby, but it was getting to be more than I could stand.

As if in answer to my prayers. Lieutenant Salter came suddenly through the door. Glenna told her what I wanted, and she immediately came over to where I was.

"Why didn't you tell me?" she asked with much concern.

"I thought I could fight it," I said. I told her how for months I had been trying to build up a nerve block against the pain.

"I'll get the O.D. and we'll have you examined in the morning to see what's wrong with you," she said.

"I don't want the O.D.," I sobbed. "I want either Captain Giest or Captain Kingston. I don't care which one."

She went out and in a very few minutes returned with Captain Giest. He looked me over carefully and asked me where I hurt.

"Our friend Louie Kingston knows about this, doesn't he, young lady?" he asked.

"Yes, but he's good at keeping promises," I said.

"The thing to do is to strap her back firmly with adhesive," he explained to Lieutenant Salter. "Let her rest in bed for a couple of days to give this thing a chance to get over the acute stage. Then maybe we can find out what is wrong with her. I suggest a hypodermic right now to relieve her pain."

They soon had me strapped so firmly I couldn't move from my waist down, and as I seemed to feel better on my face, they left me that way. Glenna came back presently with the hypo and gave it to me, and after a short while I hurt less and finally went to sleep. I wakened after a while to find Glenna dozing as she sat beside me. I woke her up and sent her to her own bed after she had helped me to turn over onto my back. Louise took a turn watching out for me, and next time I dropped off to sleep it was late forenoon before I awakened again. Little Edna Atkins managed to find enough hot water somewhere to give me a bed bath, and they wouldn't allow me to get up until Captain Giest had seen me again. Such luxury! I felt as though I was being spoiled very much indeed, as the ache had pretty well subsided by now. Shortly before chow time the good Captain arrived. He smiled at me as he came down the length of the barracks to my bedside.

"Well, chicken," he said, "they have you down for the count this time, haven't they? I knew sooner or later it would come to this. I also knew it was the only way you ever would give in and tell somebody about it. It's really been troubling both Kingston and myself for some time. But we both had a lot of respect for that temper of yours. And after he told you he wouldn't turn you in for sick call, we just waited for such a letdown as you had last night. We were watching you do your laundry out there, and Louis said then he bet you would pay for it."

I turned over and he made a more thorough examination than he had made the night before, because now I could stand the pressure of his hands. He decided I was to stay in bed for another forty-eight hours, although of course I protested vigorously.

The forty-eight hours passed, and on the third day I was up and around, but taking it mighty easy, for I was in actual terror lest the pain should return. There began to be rumors, now, about our moving. I was resting on the bed in the afternoon when Lieutenant Salter came into the, barracks looking worried. She came down to my bed and sat on the foot of it. She looked at me a minute and then said,

"Lieutenant Haskell, do you think you will be able to travel in a truck if we make a move within the next couple of days? If you can't, I shall have to leave you here with the second unit and take one of their girls in your place. I don't want to have to do that. Now what do you think?"

My heart had dropped a mile while she was talking, and when she finished, I said,

"Lieutenant Salter, when the outfit is ready to move I shall be ready to move with it." My fingers were crossed, but luckily she didn't notice.

At chow that noon we received orders to be ready to move at 5:00 p.m. Everybody exchanged glances because that meant we would be setting up again in blackout, and it was not an easy job. It also meant we were evidently going into an area that wasn't safe to be entering in the daytime— which might, in turn, mean almost anything.

Promptly at five that afternoon we started off again in a truck, but this time I was allowed to ride in the cab, and my good friend Mac bolstered me up with aspirin and codeine for the trip so it wasn't too bad, although I must admit that when we arrived I knew we had come from somewhere. I wondered what it would look like in daylight…

CHAPTER TWELVE: We Make a Strategic Withdrawal

As I OPENED the door of the cab to get out, there stood faithful Louise waiting to help me. Together we got my equipment off my shoulders, and then we stumbled off in search of Lieutenant Salter to see what was expected of us. As we followed the general direction of voices in the dark, we heard Major Mackenbrock say,

"There will be a ward tent set up as temporary shelter for the girls. We'll want to get them under canvas for the night. The enlisted men will put their bedding rolls in, and they can sleep on the ground. They may have to do it many times before this is over."

"Yes, sir," replied the Chief Nurse. "In the meantime I'll get the girls together so there'll be no confusion."

When the Major left, she turned to us and said,

"You girls remain here, and I'll round up the others. Then, when Sergeant Roberts is ready to feed us, we can eat quickly and get into the tent out of the way while the rest of the hospital is being set up."

It was cold there in the dark, and we didn't much care who knew it. I was doing my own share of griping when a voice out of heaven — or so it seemed — called out,

"Is Ruth Haskell here?"

"I'm right here, sir, what is it?" I asked, recognizing the voice of Captain Henry Carney of Boston.

"You are to come over into the cook tent where it is warmer. We can't have you becoming sick again." He came forward and took my arm, and together we started off down across the compound.

"The luck of the Irish!" I heard one girl say as we left the group of nurses.

"This is awfully nice of you, sir," I commented. "I really would have been all right out there with the others."

"After all, we New Englanders must stick together," was his whispered reply.

I sat down on a packing box in a corner of the tent where I would be out of the way, and the heat from the field ovens certainly felt good. Somebody brought me a canteen cup full of hot coffee, and after I had finished drinking it, I stayed around and watched the efficient way in which those boys in the cook tent got ready to care for some three hundred stomachs. It didn't seem any time before chow was prepared and people began coming through the line. Afterward I was just beginning to feel warm and comfortable when Louise came up to tell me that the tent was ready and that we were to go at once to bed. I thanked Captain Carney and the boys for their thoughtfulness, and she and I departed. When we arrived at the tent, I saw she had already unstrapped my bedding roll, so that all I had to do was to take off my overcoat and put it over the top of the roll for cover, remove my shoes, and crawl inside.

I twisted and turned and was generally uncomfortable, and once in the night I awoke to find myself lying under the stars. The guy ropes had apparently not been fastened, neither had all the tent pegs been driven in. In my sleep I must have wiggled under the wall of the tent, and I opened my eyes to find the guard standing over me laughing.

"Ma'am, I think you'd better crawl back inside. I'd hate to have to report you A.W.O.L., but at the rate you've been moving you'll be off the area by morning."

I grinned foolishly and wiggled my way back into the tent, wishing it were morning and time to get up. We were so crowded under the canvas that if I had started to get up I would have wakened everybody else. So I lay there uncomfortably until the noise from the kitchen tent reached my ears and the other girls began getting up one by one. We were amazed to find the complete hospital already set up for us as if by magic. As I stepped into the chow line with my mess kit. Captain Giest said,

"Up and at it, I see."

I smiled. "Have we any patients yet that you know of?"

"I understand there are a few blast injuries. Shell shock, we used to call it in the last war."

"Nothing else?" I said, rather surprised.

"You'll be plenty busy soon enough," he replied rather grimly.

As we were finishing our breakfast. Lieutenant Salter arrived to assign us to duty.

"I expect we'll have a good many patients before the day's out, from all I hear. Be on the alert for trouble, and if anything happens, hit the foxholes and stay put until you're told to get out."

The boys were busy now digging foxholes, and some of the girls pitched in and helped when they didn't have work in their tents to attend to. Somehow 1A was always the first to get patients, one reason being it was nearest the receiving end. When I reported on to the ward, I found my same three corpsmen giving the ambulatory patients water to wash in, and Smiley was at his usual job of shaving one of the boys. We had already kidded him that he could take up barbering after the war, but he decided he would go back to Wyoming and continue farming.

"Is everything all right, Lieutenant Haskell?" asked Corporal Krist.

"Fine, kid," I replied. "Have we any real sick ones?"

"That boy over there has just come to us from the operating room," he said, pointing to one of the cots. "He isn't awake yet. Calcaterra is staying with him until he reacts from the anesthesia. His cheeks were pretty well blown away, and he has a bullet hole through the roof of his mouth. He'll be pretty sick when he comes around, I imagine. Got too close to a 37 millimeter, and it certainly didn't do him any good. The others are not so bad, though there are a couple of bad burns among them."

I passed along the tent, speaking to the boys and asking their names and organizations. As I had suspected, there were a good many from the First Division groups. One lad I spoke to apparently didn't hear me, for he paid no attention to what I was trying to say. There was a set sort of expression on his face and no reaction to what was happening around him. I wondered if he could be deaf, and I went back to the improvised desk to look up the record. But before I could find it, there was the sound of a plane overhead, and although I recognized it as one of our own, the poor devil I had just left apparently didn't. He threw back the covers and started to nm out of the tent.

"Krist, Calcaterra, Smiley, stop that boy!" I cried. "Don't let him get outdoors!"

Just as he reached the tent flap, Krist caught one of his arms and Smiley the other.

"Let me go," screamed the boy hysterically. "Can't you hear them? Planes! Dozens of planes! The slit trenches, quick, before they get us! Quick, I tell you, and everything will be all right."

"You are all right, pal," said Corporal Krist, quietly. "That baby is one of ours. Nothing's going to happen. What say we go back and you get into bed and rest?"

Talking to him as one might to a child. Corporal Krist finally got him into bed. He was a great strapping man of six feet and probably weighed over two hundred pounds. But he had no more control over his nervous system than a baby. The actual shell injuries were horrible enough, but this kind seemed even more tragic. As I passed along the tent and back toward the desk, one of the soldiers stopped me.

"Nurse, would you believe it that I've been in the same company for months with that man? He was one of the best soldiers we had until a couple of days ago. Then, suddenly, he went off the handle during a bombing. He jumped up out of his foxhole and began shaking his fist at the planes and cursing them. And he's been that way ever since at the sound of a motor overhead. I'd rather be like this than like he is."

The lad speaking had just had his leg amputated below the knee and had lost three fingers from his right hand. I had to blink fast to keep back the tears which filled my eyes at sight of him.

Before the day was out, we really were busy, and I hardly knew what it was to feel rested for hours on end. The girls were all tired and a bit on the irritable side at times, but all in all pretty good soldiers. Many planes went over us toward sundown, and we could hear the sound of their bombs and know that something had been destroyed ruthlessly.

A few days later Lieutenant Salter returned from Corps Headquarters in the town with news that she had been bombed, and we got her to tell us about it.

"The bombs began falling around me," she said, "and I guess I didn't move fast enough, because a young sergeant pushed me into a foxhole and planked his helmet down hard onto my head. The explosions were terrific, and we never knew where a bomb would land next. After the planes passed over, my savior apologized and helped me out again, but at least I learned a lesson, and that was to move and move fast. They made a direct hit on the railroad junction just out of town, which evidently was their objective." She smiled and then added, "But, no kidding, it was too close for comfort!"

The next day when it came time to get up, I could hardly crawl out of my bedding roll. Louise helped me get straightened out and gave me a good telling off.

"Now don't be simple and try to work when you're feeling like this. Why don't you stay in your tent today and give your back some rest?"

"Oh, I'll be all right as soon as I walk a bit," I assured her. "It's just that I'm stiff with the cold, I think."

After chow I went down to the ward to go on duty. When Corporal Krist saw me, he looked cross enough to bite.

"What made you come to work if you didn't feel good? We don't want you sick again."

"I'm all right, fella," I said. "When I have to give up, I promise to let you know. What do you say we feed these hungry hounds now and skip it?"

But as the day progressed I felt worse, and when it came time to go off duty I went willingly. I slept very little during the night; and when morning came, I was dreading the thought of getting up. Mary Meyer arrived at the tent with a very disgruntled look on her face.

"Ruthie," said she, "we're both to become patients for a while. Lieutenant Salter said I was to tell you to get your things together. You're going to be admitted, and they want to give you a series of tests to see if they can find out what's the matter with you. Somebody reported you were limping when you didn't think anybody was watching you, so that's that. As for me, I have an infection in my face from picking a pimple under my chin. Captain Kingston says I have to go to bed and have hot compresses on it. So we might as well go together. I'll go to the tent and get my things and come back for you. Will you be ready?"

I had been thinking all the while she was talking to me, and somehow or other I was obliged to admit to myself I was about at the end of my rope.

"Yes," I said, "I'll be ready. But I hope they find out what's wrong soon so I can get back to duty."

In a little while she and I were installed in a ward tent all by ourselves.

Helen Molony was to be our nurse by day and Louise Miller by night. That pleased us because Helen and Mary were tentmates, the same as Louise and I. Hot packs were started on Mary's face, and everybody and his brother came in to see me and examine me. The orthopedic man examined my back, and so did one of the surgeons, and finally Captain Giest said that due to the history I gave of having had the pain since the fall on the ship, he wanted to examine me from a neurological standpoint. He made the diagnosis that I had a ruptured intervertebral disc (which later was proved to be true), and I was ordered to stay in bed and rest.

Soon the hospital began to fill up again, but no amount of pleading on the part of either Mary or myself would let them put us back to work. They soon needed the tent we were in, so a small wall tent was set up for us down in the hospital area, the opening of which faced on the highway. I began to wonder what was happening up at the front, for all day long there seemed to be a steady flow of patients into the hospital, and almost as soon as they were treated they would be transported back to the evacuation unit in the rear. To be there, where I could watch all the activity in camp and not be a part of it, irked me considerably; but I fully realized there wasn't a thing I could do about it.

Finally Mary prevailed upon them to let her get up and help for a bit at least, but no amount of coaxing on my part would get me out with her. As I lay there watching through the tent flap, huge caravans of camels were going past — not at their usual lazy gait, but at full speed — being urged on by the Arabs who rode them and ran alongside. This seemed strange in itself, for I had never before seen a camel break out of a walk, and I knew that something was happening at the front. Soon there began to be a steady stream of peasant folk headed in the same direction, the men riding on the burros, as was the custom there, and the women carrying their worldly goods on their heads. Some of the burros were hauling little cart-like affairs which seemed to be piled high with household furnishings.

I was consumed with curiosity, and there wasn't a soul around I could ask what it was all about. I didn't dare try to get up, for I was getting steadily weaker, and even my appetite — this of all things! — had begun to desert me. As I lay there, pondering the strange goings on, I could see that nearly all the patients were being evacuated and started on their way down the same highway. Everyone wore the same worried, grim expression as they hurriedly crossed the compound from one tent to another. I thought: If only someone would come this way so I could ask a few questions.

As I continued to watch the road, truck load after truck load of infantry rolled by, the guns on their cabs pointed skyward, the men all armed to the teeth. Then tanks followed, and the sound of the firing to the north seemed to be nearer than it had been for several days. When even the half tracks, with the 105's and 155's mounted on them, rolled past, I really began to be concerned. What under the name of the Lord was going on up front? To me it all spelled the same terrible word: retreat. The Nazis were pushing us back!

Just when I thought I couldn't stand it any longer, Major Mackenbrock hurried past the flap of my tent on his way to headquarters.

"Major Mackenbrock, sir," I yelled. "Does all that down on the highway really mean what I think?"

He didn't hear at first, and when he good-naturedly poked his head inside the tent, I repeated my question. He turned and watched the highway for a minute, with the many tanks and half tracks still going by, and when he looked at me again his face was deathly serious.

"Yes, Lieutenant Haskell, I'm afraid it means just that. But don't be frightened, you'll be taken care of. We've already evacuated most of the patients, but I wanted to keep you with the unit. We'll all go back together when the time comes."

"Have you a cigarette, sir?" I asked.

He tossed me a pack. I took one out and tossed it back.

"How do you feel?" He stepped in and gave me a light.

"Now that I know we're going to see this through together, why, I feel fine, sir."

"Good girl," he said and hurried away toward headquarters.

I thought: Haskell, this is a darned fine time for you to be flat on your back — when they need you more than ever.

Most of the nurses dropped in for a minute, from time to time, to see if I was all right, and then Sergeant Hurley brought me something to eat. He was a little indignant that I was alone, but I told him I didn't mind since the girls were all very busy helping to pack the equipment and get the hospital down so we could move as much of it as possible if and when the quartermaster arrived to transport us. He smiled, patted me on the cheek awkwardly, and then, in an embarrassed manner, muttered something about my being a "good soldier" and took off as though the devil were chasing him. Not long after that Sergeant Michael Gregory stuck his head in the tent and asked if there was anything I wanted, and cursed a little because we didn't have transportation.

"As far as the men are concerned," he said, "I don't mind so much. They can look after themselves more or less. But with you girls, it's another matter. I always said this was too far front for the women. As long as we are going ahead, it's all right. It's this backing up business that's dangerous."

Soon Miller arrived to stay with me. She told me our living quarters were all down and that she had packed and rolled my bedding roll and taken care of my baggage in general.

"The Chief doesn't know if we'll be able to take baggage or not. It all depends on how much transportation comes for us. But it won't hurt to have it ready just in case."

By this time I was getting jittery because of my utter uselessness in the emergency. I began wondering, too, how the second unit was making out. In a way they were nearer than we were, and I knew we were near enough!

There was a flurry of dust, now, down near headquarters, and an M.P. came in with a flourish on his motor bike. He dismounted and started shouting so loud we could hear every word.

"What in hell are you people doing here? There's nothing between you and the enemy but the rear guard!"

I heard the CO. tell him it was a matter of transportation, and he left in a bigger hurry than he arrived. I don't know how or why, but it wasn't long thereafter that two trucks rolled into the compound. Some mattresses were piled onto the floor of one, and the few remaining patients, and the nurses, were piled into the rear of it. Lieutenant Salter arrived at the door of the tent just then and said,

"Lieutenant Miller, get Lieutenant Haskell dressed as best you can, and be quick about it. I'll take her in the cab of the truck with the driver. I'm sorry, Haskell, I know it's been hell for you, but there isn't any other way out of it. We had hoped to evacuate you by ambulance, but there's no time for that now. Keep your chin up. I'll call for you in ten minutes."

"Yes, ma'am," I said just as a thundering explosion from not far away made the ground vibrate under my cot. I tried to sit up, but my last dose of codeine was still having effect and I was woozy as a drunk. Finally we got me into my slacks and sweater and overcoat and shoes, and then Sergeant Gregory and the Chaplain helped me to my feet and, between them, got me into the cab of the truck. The other truck was being used to transport our surgical equipment, and then both were to return for the rest of the outfit.

We pulled slowly down onto the highway between two tanks. They were wheeling right along, and presently we were, too. All hell was popping to the rear of us, and the treads of the tank ahead would shoot blue sparks out into the air two or three feet when it would slow around a curve — it was traveling so fast. Talk about excitement, this was it! I was so excited, and I guess nervous at the same time, that I almost forgot about myself until — of all things — I began to be sick to my stomach from the sedation! When I told the Chief, she looked nonplussed for a minute and then said,

"We haven't time to stop now. Here, have a helmet!" And with those words, she passed me the metal part of her helmet, keeping the liner on her head.

Until one has heaved into a helmet in the cab of a truck traveling sixty-five miles an hour, one has never been sick to the stomach. When I had finished, she rolled down the window of the cab, turned the helmet away from the wind and let her go. Then she calmly poured a little water out of her canteen and into the helmet, sloshed it around for a second, emptied it and put the thing back on her head. It was that simple!

As we put more space between us and the area we had vacated, there was less sound from the battle area, and we began to breathe with a little more ease. I was still terribly worried about our officers and enlisted men, and hoped they would get out all right. They were too darned nice people to have anything happen to them, and I really prayed for them that night.

After riding for something like three hours, we passed through a sleepy little town. The driver sighed audibly.

"What is it, soldier?" I asked.

"We haven't much farther to go, ma'am," he said. "And I thank God for that. I don't mind hauling equipment, but I'm damned if I like being responsible for patients and women. We're too good a target, and I'm not kidding you."

I replied that as far as I was concerned, he could stop at any time. But we rolled on through the town and to the outskirts. Just ahead of us were many more ward tents than I had ever seen set up in any one area.

"Is that where we are going?" I asked. "I understood we were to join the second unit. There are a lot more tents there than they would have."

"I think there's another hospital unit with them," answered the driver unenthusiastically.

Just then we drove up in front of the tent marked headquarters. The truck rolled to a stop, and Lieutenant Salter got out and went in. It didn't seem she had been gone more than a minute when she arrived back at the door with Mary Francis of the second unit.

"Come on. Lieutenant Haskell," she said. "Lieutenant Francis will take you to one of the night nurse's cots, and you can get into bed. We'll try to get you more comfortably located in the morning. There are nine hundred patients here under these tents. The evacuation has joined Second Unit to take care of the casualties from the retreat. I guess it's been pretty horrible all over this section. We have been busy, but nothing like as busy as this group."

"How's the fighting going?" I asked, expecting the worst.

"Our forces are holding them at least on this flank. Let's hope they hold until our men get out of the other flank and join us. I'd feel a lot better if I thought there was something up ahead of them, but we know there isn't."

As she finished speaking, Lieutenant Francis came up, and together they helped me out of the cab. I found I could hardly stand. We walked up the road just a little and then crossed into one of the wall tents, and I crawled into bed. I was utterly exhausted and fell asleep almost immediately. I guess if Jerry had stood there with a tommy gun in his hand, he would have had to let me sleep before he could have taken me prisoner!

I wakened next morning to the sound of mess kits and the voices of people standing in the chow line. I managed to get to my feet and was standing in the door of the tent when Vaughn Fisher came into sight.

"Where do you think you are going?" she asked. "Get back into that bed. I've been sent to see that you get something to eat and that you are made a little more comfortable. Did you ever see a bigger chow line?" she added.

"No, I certainly never did. Tell me about yourselves. How did you make out, and how long have you been here?" I asked.

"We moved and set up twice," she explained. "The first time, we had a great many patients and were able to move them all, but it was too near the Germans for comfort, and they sent us farther back. That's when the evacuation joined us, and it's a good thing they did because we'd never have been able to handle all the casualties by ourselves. As it is, there are a great many of them sleeping on cots out in the field across the road from here. The sickest ones are under cover. They're planning to evacuate as many as possible by plane down to the station and general hospitals at the coast."

Just then one of the enlisted men arrived and called out that he had my breakfast. She asked him to bring it in, and of all things — trust the Americans to be different! The night before, we retreat from the enemy; and so help me, the next morning we have pancakes for breakfast!

As I ate, I asked Vaughn Fisher what the patients had to say about the retreat and if the casualties were large. She replied that the patients were experiencing their usual sense of anger and frustration when anything goes wrong, and that there had been a good many casualties, but that all in all the morale seemed to stand up pretty well. Suffering a setback seemed to have served one purpose at least: it had convinced the men that being Yanks was not enough, and that they must prove themselves smarter than the other fellow if they were not to be surprised and chased back again. We paid dearly in both men and equipment for the retreat at Kasserine Pass, but it was a lesson well learned, and perhaps one we had to learn before moving across Tunisia to final victory in the African campaign. It made seasoned fighters out of green American soldiers and shattered any illusions we might have had about our own invincibility.

I thanked Vaughn for her help, and as she left, I dropped off to sleep. The next thing I knew, one of our medical officers was saying,

"She's in here, boys. Move her carefully. She has a bad back, and it sure caught hell last night. She's to go into the ward tent with the rest of the nurses from her group. Put her into the bed by the stove, because shell be laid up for a few days, at least."

"Hello, there," I cried. "What's news from back yonder?"

"The men are all right," the medical officer assured me, "but they're not all here yet. They got out none too soon, though, for as the last load drove away from the old hospital site they were digging in there, and that was the front. Now, how do you like that?"

The boys put me carefully onto the litter, and soon I was installed in bed with my own group of girls. They certainly babied and spoiled me, and I loved every minute of it. What I didn't know then was that they were being so darned nice to me because I was to go on the plane the next morning to be evacuated down to the coast for treatment. I guess they thought I would raise a rumpus when I knew it, and so they were outdoing themselves being kind. I was relaxed and happy for the first time in hours when Lieutenant Salter came in and announced that the boys had been able to get every last piece of luggage away from the camp site in the trucks — a feat that had been nothing short of remarkable under the circumstances. She walked over and sat down on the front of my bed.

"How do you feel. Lieutenant Haskell? I have something to tell you that I know you won't like." And then she sprang the bad news. "Arrangements have been made to fly you back to Oran for treatment. If they're able to help you, you'll eventually be returned to us. If not, you'll be sent on to the States. Believe me, I wish you might remain here. But it's a case of must, and I know you'll understand it as such."

I guess I must have understood, for somehow the rumpus they were all expecting failed to materialize. Maybe I was too weak to argue. Anyway, I looked at Lieutenant Salter through badly blurred eyes and said simply, "I'll try to be a good sport about this thing. But you needn't think it isn't going to hurt." I brushed a tear aside quickly and asked for a cigarette. I was feeling lower than an earthworm at that moment.

The rest of the day passed somehow, and there was a strained feeling among the girls and myself. I think they realized, as I did, that I wouldn't be joining them again, even though we were trying to kid each other into believing I would.

Early the next morning I sent for Janet Pettingill, but she was busy. She lived in Gardiner, Maine, just six miles from my home, and since we had both been overseas, her mother and mine had struck up quite a friendship. I wanted to tell her not to write her mother that I was ill, because I hadn't told my parents anything about it and I didn't want my Mum to be scared to death hearing it from another source. Finally I got someone to leave a message for her to that effect, and then after a few hurried goodbyes to my closest friends I started out with Louise, Lieutenant Salter, and Chaplain Groves for the airport at Youkes Le-Baine, where I was to be put on board a plane for the coast. I blinked hard to keep the tears back, but in the end I had to let them come. Nobody paid any attention to me, and in a minute I had myself under control again. Louise got on the plane while they strapped the litter in place, and then, with her shy little smile, she repeated her words of the night of invasion:

"Goodbye, Yankee. Take good care of yourself!" A quick kiss on my cheek and she was gone.

The Chief and Chappy, as we called him, bade me a quick goodbye, and then I was alone, the only passenger on the plane.

There was a rush of the motor and then we slowly rolled along the runway, gathering speed until we were in the air. For a few minutes after the take-off, I watched out of the window until our ward tents at the hospital area were reduced to tiny pinpoints on the ground below. They might have been sleeping flies on some great patchwork quilt that covered the whole earth as far as eye could see.

I guess I must have looked as depressed as I felt, for the navigator came along and began to talk to me. He was a solid, nerveless-looking chap, with warm, friendly eyes.

"It's tough luck, girl," he said, laying a hand on my shoulder. "But you'll be back."

"I wish I were sure of it," I said. "You don't know what it's like running out on them. They're mighty real people, our boys!"

I felt his grip tighten on my shoulder. "You bet your sweet life they are," he agreed. After that he went away and I fell asleep.

I was held for several weeks at Casablanca, awaiting a transport to the States. It was April when we docked at Staten Island, after a trip that was happily uneventful. The sound of the bell buoys as we came into the blacked-out harbor was music to my ears, for I had not cared to meet Jerry on the water in my helpless condition. I was admitted next day to Halloran

Hospital, where ultimately I underwent surgery on my spine. A long and tiresome convalescence followed. . . .

Now, as I walk down the corridor of the efficiently managed hospital at Camp Gordon, wearing again my stiff white uniform and cap, walking straight and painlessly once again, thanks to God and an Army surgeon — and good nursing — there is only one question in my mind: When, oh, when do I go back?